# Walk Beside Me

*A Memoir of
Thelma Adams Rodgers*

T.A.R. Publishing

**Walk Beside Me**

Copyright © 2014 by Thelma A. Rodgers

All rights reserved. This book or any portion thereof may not be reproduced or used in any manner whatsoever without the express written permission of the publisher except for the use of brief quotations in a book review or scholarly journal.

Edited By: Jason T. Collins & Barbara S. Rodgers
Layout & Cover Design: Jason T. Collins
Front Cover Photo: Janice R. Collins
　*New York City, April 1974*
Back Cover Photo: Barbara S. Rodgers
　*Jimmy & Thelma's 74$^{th}$ Wedding Anniversary, September 2013*
Interior Photos: Rodgers, Collins, & Adams Family

Scripture Quotations: Holy Bible - King James Version

Printed in the United States of America

First Printing, March 2014

ISBN 978-0-578-13746-9

T.A.R. Publishing
P.O. Box 541
LaFayette, Alabama 36862

Dedicated in loving memory of my precious daughter, Edwina, who encouraged and inspired me to publish the story of my life and my collection of poems.

*Come, walk beside me*
　　*through the window of my journey.*
*Come, walk beside me*
　　*through happy times and adversity.*
*Come, walk beside me*
　　*through 96 years of experiences.*
*Come, walk beside me*
　　*through the valleys and over the hilltops.*
*God has brought me through them all,*
*For my Lord was there to walk beside me.*

As you turn each page you will understand that our loving Lord Jesus is always with us. Miracles still happen because I am one of them. We are never perfect, "But He loves us still."

I hope you have fun reading, and I wish you joy, love, and peace everlasting.

*Thelma Adams Rodgers*

# Contents

The Early Years . . . . . . . . . . . . . . . . . . . . . . Page 11

A Tribute to Papa . . . . . . . . . . . . . . . . . . . . . Page 29

The Story Continues . . . . . . . . . . . . . . . . . . Page 34

Photos . . . . . . . . . . . . . . . . . . . . . . . . . . . . . Page 75

Poetry . . . . . . . . . . . . . . . . . . . . . . . . . . . . . Page 93

Photos . . . . . . . . . . . . . . . . . . . . . . . . . . . . . Page 165

# The Early Years

On Christmas Eve 1912, Herbert Holston Adams and Parrie Lee Stanfield were married in Chambers County, Alabama. They soon settled down and started their lives on their farm in LaFayette, Alabama, and were very much in love. After only two short years, they knew they were going to be parents, and they prepared for the event with much joy and anticipation. On March 8, 1914, they gave birth to a beautiful baby girl, whom they named Edna. Everyone petted her so much until she thought she was the boss, and some of the kinfolk even began calling her "Miss Bossy." Three years later on April 14, 1917, I was born, and they named me Thelma. The old house where I was born looked almost like a barn, but I don't suppose it mattered in the long run because I've stayed fairly healthy my entire life. My sister and I didn't favor much; she took after the Adams side of the family and I took after the Stanfields. Edna had a more outward personality than I did, and she had curly hair whereas mine was straight as a stick. Looking back now, I think I always envied her beauty. She wasn't an outdoor person like I was, but that didn't bother me because I was a busy little bee.

There were twelve brothers and sisters in Papa's family. I recall his saying that he couldn't believe he ever saw his mother without a baby in her lap. With twelve children in the family you would almost have to choose one to be your playmate. My grandmother was very small, never weighing over seventy-nine pounds. Her name was Olivia Amanda Melvena McClendon.

My dad's father and family lived close to the river, and sometimes the younger children would go down to the river alone. I guess Granny had so many kids that she could not keep up with all of them. One day their dad went to town, and when he came home he brought Papa a little hat. Papa was so proud of that hat, and every time he and his brother went down to the river Papa would wear it proudly. One day while standing on the old ferry that carried people across the river, his brother snatched off Papa's hat and threw it in the river. Papa said he almost jumped in to get it because he could hardly stand to see his little hat floating down the river. I'm sure now that an angel was standing there by him and kept him from deciding to jump into the river. If he had, he would have drowned because he could not swim, and the river current was too swift.

My dad was a handsome man; he was over six feet tall with curly hair and could really make a banjo talk. He would call square dances and say, "swing her to the right, swing her to the left, swing your partner, promenade all." He was the life of the party on many occasions. My parents would take Edna and me sometimes to these gatherings, and we soon learned to square dance. It was all fun, and at the time we were young teenagers. I remember my mom being so petite and a very loving and sweet soul. She taught us not to gossip. She said, "Be a good friend, and you will have good friends."

There were seven children in Mom's family. Unfortunately, their mother died when the kids were very young. Grandpa could not raise them alone so he let other members of the family have them. Mama and Aunt Maggie got to stay together because one family wanted both of them. When they eventually married, they ironically married brothers. Papa said he knew he was his dad's favorite among the children because

Parrie Lee Adams (Mama)

every time Papa had a date his dad would say, "Herbert, go and pick the best horse and buggy." Grandpa liked the girl that my dad dated – my future mom. I know he picked the sweetest girl in the world. Papa would sit and tell us about his growing up years, as I often call them. They didn't get to play as much as we did and learned the value of hard work at an early age.

My most favorite time of year was the summer time. I could stay with my dad in the field. I would follow behind him in his tracks as he plowed, and quite literally was his little shadow. The soft dirt felt good to my bare feet, and I would take him cool water to drink after he spent hours in the blazing sun. He often would sit down to rest a bit and talk to me. I would sit there and rake some soft dirt over my feet and make frog houses, only for them to be torn down later by the plow. When we were ready to stop working for the evening, he would let me ride the ole mule home. Sometimes the mule didn't want me to ride her, and she would throw me. Dad was determined that I would ride and have fun despite the mule's temperament. My dad really loved me. He didn't intend for an ole mule to mistreat me!

So many times while working in the field, I'd see a grasshopper come along. I was so fascinated by those little creatures. When I saw a big one with blue behind his long hind legs, I would go after him. The rest of the folks working would stop and watch me run – they knew the chase was on, and I wouldn't give up until I caught the grasshopper. I'd throw down my hoe, snatch off my bonnet, and run like crazy. After my catch I went back where the workers were, and I said, "Well, I caught the ole rascal." One little black lady still propped on her hoe said, "She sho did." Catching grasshoppers was one of the most fascinating playtimes I remember having. I would build a little rock house and feed the grasshopper some grass and watch him

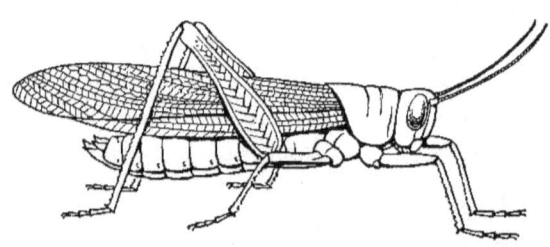

eat like crazy. I would soon let him out of this jail though because I knew there were plenty more in the wide open fields, and that he should roam free. It was a long time before I eventually gave up my grasshopper catching. No child ever had a happier childhood than I.

All my growing up years our family stayed a close, loving family. We shared play time and work time. My sister did not like to play with dolls like I often did. I had a little doll that I named Fred Scott because my dad had a good friend by that name, and I thought that was the prettiest name I had ever heard. I was only about three years old at the time. That little doll went with me to the field and even to the storm pit. My dad always dug a storm pit wherever we lived to keep us safe during the often unpredictable weather. One day Dad brought home a little Jack Russell dog, and we named her Tee Wee. Tee Wee was so adorable and smart – she made the perfect companion. Edna didn't like dogs, so Tee Wee and I became inseparable play buddies. I could talk to her, and she seemed to understand. She would sit straight up with her front feet straight out in front of her until you told her, "Down."

At this time we were living in an old log house not very far from the bank of Hootalocco Creek. We loved that old creek. We could fish or just play in the water. It had a road running through the shallow part but never a bridge. I guess the county was too poor to build one. We also had a pathway that went from our house to my Uncle Roscoe Adams' house; he was my dad's brother. The path went from our house across the field through a little patch of woods. We liked to go there because he had a big family and kids who were our age. But one day Dad said that he and Tee Wee were going to see Roscoe and talk awhile. When he started home, a fit came over Tee Wee. She started running as fast as she could and foaming terribly at the mouth. My dad started running after her. When he got in sight of our house he started calling mom as loud as he could, saying, "Don't let that baby touch Tee Wee!" He was saying it over and over. By the time he reached home, I had already run out and took Tee Wee in my arms. That's what my dad was afraid of happening. He knew how much I loved that little dog.

He was completely exhausted and out of breath, but he told mom to run a tub of water, jerk off my slimy clothes and bathe me quickly, or I was in danger of getting rabies. My parents were so frightened; they were standing on the edge of time. All they had was time. Would their little girl die, or would God intervene that she might live? Mama grabbed a basin of

Edna, Thelma & Tee Wee

water, put me in it and almost scrubbed the skin off me. What more could they do now? They waited so helpless, but they knew the Great Almighty was always standing on high to help His own. So after a few days, I was not sick with rabies and neither was Tee Wee. My parents believed in miracles.

Unfortunately, one day my uncle came along in his car and ran over her and she died. My heart was broken and to this day I've never loved another dog as much as I did my Tee Wee. One thing funny about that old log house – we moved to another place, and after two or three years we moved back into the same log house. I never knew why!

Around this time, I was eight years old and my sister was eleven, and we knew that our mother was going to have another baby. We knew what our duties were and what was expected of us from our parents. My sister and I did the extra work in the fields and home while our dad plowed the fields. Our mother could not work in the field, so it was left to us to pull up the slack. We chaps, as dad called us, had to learn fast and take over with the tasks we could handle. We were very smart and quick to catch on to the tasks at hand. We waited anxiously for our baby brother to be born. He was born May 9, 1925, and my parents named him Joe Floyd. I knew dad was glad to finally have a son. He was so cute, and I remember not being able to wait to hold him. I often took care of him while mom did some of the housework. He was a good baby, and I loved him with all my heart.

Time passed, and I remember hearing my parents talking about the 'olden days.' They told me about the horrific epidemic flu that killed so many people. My parents had it, and so did I when I was only a few months old – they thought I wouldn't live. They told me about this old black lady coming by to see how we were doing. She saw how sick we were and stayed with us throughout our entire sickness. She told my mother that she was going to hold me because if she laid me down I would certainly die. They called her Aunt Gussie, and as I think back now, I believe she was Heaven sent. Fortunately, Edna never contracted the flu, and we all recovered and remained in good health in the years that followed. My dad talked about that flu many times!

Aunt Gussie wore a beautiful eighteen-carat gold wide band ring. My mother once said to her, "Aunt Gussie, that sure is a pretty ring you have on," and Aunt Gussie said, "Do you want this ring?" When mom said yes, Aunt Gussie just pulled it off and gave it to mom. She wore that ring from then until she gave it away. One day my daughter asked my mom if she would will her that ring when she passed. Mom pulled it off her finger at that moment and handed it to my daughter, Edwina, and said, "you better take it now." That ring is still in our family today.

As I mentioned before, when I was eight years old and my sister was eleven, we had to do all of the work in the field while our dad plowed. Our little brother had just been born so mom had to tend to the new baby, but we learned fast and did what we were told. I remember this project like it was yesterday. Papa gave each of us a bucket with fertilizer in them and told us to go over to the watermelon patch and fertilize it well; he said, "Be sure you put it between the vines." They had just started little short runs on them so it was an ideal time to fertilize. Just as we started this task, Edna said to me, "I am going to make mine grow faster than your row." She shouldn't have said that; the more she put around hers, the more I put around mine! When fertilizer touches leaves or vines of plants, they die, but God's hands were upon those tender watermelon vines, so they lived – another miracle.

We never told dad that his watermelon patch looked like white snow mounds all over. It was a sight to see, and we carefully packed the fertilizer around the vines, covering almost every inch of exposed dirt. To our surprise the vines didn't die; they actually made more watermelons than ever before. I know God had His hand on those little  tender vines – He does the impossible. Our dad would tell mom at night, "The chaps did real good today."

I have talked about how my sister, Edna, and I had to work in the field, but most of the time we didn't work alone. I remember one fall during cotton-picking time, my dad fell off his wagon and broke four ribs. He could not work at all, but on

bright moon shiny nights all teenagers in the community would come and help us pick cotton. We soon had all the crop gathered. What a blessing! I still think about it. Of course, we had some fun picking because somebody was always telling something funny. My dad got well and could not thank those kids enough.

We had a good neighbor who had a son and a daughter, named Hassell and Jewel Childers. They were about the same age as Edna and me. Our dad told us that if we finished working a certain piece of ground on Saturday morning, we could have Saturday evening to do whatever we wanted to do. So watch out creek, here we come! We had all kinds of fun because you could look over the hill and you would see Hassell and Jewel come running with their own hoes to help us. What a blessing that was; they were our special help.

We also had two cousins, Ernest and Kirkland Adams, who spent so many weekends with us. They loved my dad and mom. We became more like brothers and sisters than just cousins. They were always ready to help us work, play games, or help plan parties. We had a big white yard to mark off games, such as hopscotch, spinning the bottle, hide and seek, ring around the roses. We always had to keep our yards swept clean. Oh no, no grass must be found growing in the yards. How things have changed.

One of the last good friends I grew up with was Hazelwood Childers. I thought he was the cutest boy I ever saw, and we stayed sweethearts a long time. He gave me a beautiful valentine one year, and I still have that valentine in a scrapbook. His family was at one time our neighbors, but they moved from the country to the city. I was seventeen, and he was eighteen when he passed away. It was such a shock. Even though I had not seen him for a long time, I did get to go to view the body. When I walked in their house, his mother jumped up to meet me and said, "Lord, here comes his kid sweetheart." I really loved the family. It was a sad day for me, but I later married the sweetest man on earth!

In the early days it seemed that we had more bad weather and severe storms than we do now. I remember one afternoon a mighty hailstorm came just as our cotton crop was beginning to bloom. The lightning flashed, the thunder roared, and the hail cut our cotton stalks off almost to the ground. We always went in the storm pit when a bad cloud came overhead. This time when we came out of the storm pit, and looked at the hail torn field, we were terrified at what the storm had done. I still remember how my mother cried. Shortly after the storm a beautiful rainbow flashed across the sky. We knew then that God always takes care of our troubles and that He would see us through the winter. The cotton crop was truly a miracle when it started growing back, and we were able to make one bale of cotton that year.

We didn't always live in the same area of the country, but wherever we moved we always seemed to have good friends and neighbors. All the young kids liked to come to our house to play. Sometimes my parents joined in to help us all have a good time. My dad would play the banjo, and we all would attempt to dance or sing. Sometimes dad would 'buck dance' – a sight to behold if there ever was one. He had lots of rhythm, and he was a good entertainer. Some people wanted him to teach them how to dance. Sometimes on moon-shining nights we would go to the yard and play games – hop scotch, marbles, pitching horse shoes, or jumping rope.

As we grew to become young teenagers, we began to look for more daring fun. We lived close to Pigeon Roost Creek. We would go down to this creek and find a tall tree with a muscadine vine growing into the tree. We would then cut the vine off at the desired length and swing across the creek. We didn't care if we fell into the creek because that was also fun. We continued our vine swinging for many years. In fact, some of our friends had begun to date, and we called those who just casually saw one another 'sweethearts' back in those days.

The Great Depression began in 1929 when I was only twelve years old. I remember hearing folks talk about the bad times. They would often say, "What are we going to do?" So many banks had to close, and millions of people lost their jobs. Those who had some savings in the bank ended up losing it all. Herbert Hoover was a Republican, and he was elected President in 1929. People will always blame Hoover for the depression, but things were already going poorly as he won the presidential election. I remember how much my dad disliked Herbert Hoover, but looking back now I suppose he wasn't all to blame. He just failed knowing how to best carry on or enact government policies that could pull the country out of economic hardship. Franklin D. Roosevelt, a Democrat, ran against Hoover and won the presidential election in 1932. Roosevelt started a program called The New Deal, and it helped people to have better hope for the economy and their own personal finances. There were millions of people out of work, and they had neither money nor job. My dad helped build a concrete bridge during The New Deal over Pigeon Roost Creek that still stands today.

I guess the reason the depression didn't affect us so severely was because we were already living in poverty. My dad had no money in the bank, and he only owned a one-horse wagon and a mule. He never owned an automobile through- out his entire life. Since my dad farmed, we spent all summer planning for the coming winter. We grew our own vegetables, and mom canned many of them. We had a cow for milk, hog for meat, chickens for eggs, and we would heel in potatoes, and dad would take corn to the gristmill to grind for meal. We never had luxuries like some people, but we were happy and blessed with what we did have. I remember hearing one man say that he could never forget the depression; he remarked, "Oh yes, I climbed our persimmon tree a lot of mornings and ate my breakfast." That was both funny and sad at the same time.

My dad told me the only reason he managed to avoid being drafted into World War I was because of Edna and me.

Any married man with children was exempted. Despite this, they did call on him to consider joining, and they told him he had the best feet for running of any enlistees they had examined. My dad never went to World War I, but he lived long enough to see his son, Floyd, fight in World War II. At the time it hurt him badly to see his only son go to war, but he lived to see him come home.

The depression ended in 1939, but everything was still turbulent and times uncertain. After the Japanese attack on Pearl Harbor, manufacturing ramped back up as a result of the United States being thrust into World War II. Now in 2013, our situation seems to once again be in a 'tailspin,' and many are struggling to get by each month. Across the country things are not looking very good, and people are suffering some of the same hardships as we did during the depression. We must be praying that God will save our Nation!

During the depression we had a rolling store that came through the community once a week. It was loaded with lots of goods and items that people needed. It was a great help to a predominantly farming community that didn't have access to some items otherwise. It even sold fabric material, and I remember it was ten cents a yard. For a point of reference, it took two-and-a-half yards to make me a dress. Therefore, my dress would cost twenty-five cents, but even this small amount was hard to get during this difficult period. You could take chickens, eggs, and shelled corn to exchange for what you wanted. The man that owned this store was so nice, and we looked forward to coming to the rolling store every week. It was surprising how much his vehicle would hold, and he thought about all the kitchen items and odds and ends you wouldn't have normally thought you needed.

My sister Edna had begun to date. She met a nice, good looking young man by the name of Lowell Turnham. After dating for about a year they fell in love and got married. They were very happy together and stayed in the house with us for awhile. Soon Lowell knew that he had to find a house, get a job, and be ready to care for his family. They were expecting their first child, and they were living in an area called Beat Four at Marcoot at this time. When the baby came, it was a girl, and they named her Grace.

She was a beautiful baby, and I went and stayed with them awhile to help care for her. Lowell decided he had to find another place to live as soon as possible. His brother-in-law had bought a farm with a good house on it above Roanoke, Alabama, in a little place called Maloon. He told Lowell to move there and said it would be a good place, and Lowell heeded this advice. Lowell had never farmed, so little did he know what he was getting into. He planted a big cotton crop, and I can truly say the grass took over and almost ate them up. I had to go and help them out of this predicament and during this time Edna and I grew close to one another. We often talked about our years at home. I asked her one day if she remembered when we lived in the old log house down by Hootalocco Creek and we heard so many weird noises. She said that she vaguely remembered, and we laughed about those times.

Thelma at the House Where She Was Born

I began telling her about the night that papa heard a squeaking noise near the fireplace. He thought somebody was trying to break in the old wooden shutter. It was a plank window with hinges and a big latch to lock it, but it wasn't a very secure window. Mama pieced quilts a lot, and she kept her scissors hanging on a nail by the fireplace. That night she just hung them up, and they stayed closed for awhile. It was not until when they started to come open that they made a peculiar and creepy noise.

Papa jumped out of bed and he hardly knew what to do because he didn't have a gun. He quickly composed his thoughts and snatched a bed slat from underneath the mattress and ran to the fireplace. He hollered real loud, "If you come in here I will knock your head off!" About that time, the scissors began to open up even more. With a few coals in the fireplace he could see them shaking and he realized he was just talking to an old pair of scissors. Edna said, "I had almost forgotten about that," and we had a big laugh because moments such as these should never be lost to time.

Back in the olden days our beds just consisted of one mattress, open springs, and about four or five inch wide planks for bed slats. We didn't have fine luxuries like there are today – all these push button gadgets, refrigerators, deep freezers, microwaves, etc. If we wanted to keep our milk cool, we put it in the storm pit or lowered it down between the walls of the well. Where there's a will there's a way! We didn't have television or telephones, but we received our news from word of mouth. Despite all of these hardships people were happy. Neighbors went to sit and talk with their fellow neighbors until bed time. When one farmer got behind with his crop, other neighbors went and gave him a day's work to help.

I said to Edna, "I know none of us could ever forget this instance." One day papa said he was going to town to sell a bale of cotton. We always hated for him to go and be away from us for what seemed to be long periods of time. On many of these trips he would meet up with a buddy of his, and they would start drinking. When he left he said, "I will be back before night." He left and we thought about him all day, so when it started getting dark, and he still wasn't home we really got worried. We just sat by the fireplace and listened for a wagon to come, but no wagon and no dad came home for the night. We cried so much because we had no way to look for him. The next day he finally came home, and we asked him what had happened. He said, "They locked me up. I just walked by the jail, and I heard a man calling from a window saying, 'Hey, fellow, bring me a cigarette!' I asked the jailer several times to let me go up there and take that fellow a cigarette. He got tired of my pestering him, and he said to me, because he knew that I had been drinking, 'Man if you don't leave and go home, I am going to lock you up.' I kept pestering him, and he did lock me up." It came out in the LaFayette Sun, our local newspaper, that week, and this was the headline, "We have had a lot of people to break out of jail, but Herbert Adams is the first one we've had to break in jail." We laughed, and I said, "I think it's good sometimes to reminisce about these old times." It seemed that she and I had grown closer to each other during these reflections, and I definitely missed her not being home with us. Sometimes when my dad started drinking, he would drink too much, and it would make him sick. It bothered me a lot, and I would hug him and say, "Papa, I wish you wasn't so sick." I would bathe his face, hoping he would get better. I was a loving little thing.

I remember my dad digging storm pits wherever we lived, and if there wasn't one already there, papa would surely dig one. I remember moving to one place that already had a storm pit dug in a smoke house. We thought that was a super idea. We even put our milk in the pit because it was cooler there than in the house. During watermelon season we would put our ripe melons in the smoke house on top of the storm pit. We thought this was an ideal safe haven, but we were soon to learn it was like a set trap, waiting to be sprung.

We always had a lot of young teenagers coming to see us; my parents loved company. So one day there were several young folks at our house, and papa told us to go to the smoke house and get some watermelons to cut. We did, but the most frightening thing happened that you could ever see, but yet it was also funny. When we got to the smoke house and opened the door, Mae Lambert jumped in first. Then all of a sudden a big log that covered the pit snapped, and the whole storm pit fell in carrying all the red dirt that covered the top of the pit, all logs falling in, watermelons falling and busting open on Mae, and as she was going down, she was throwing her hands up and screaming to the top of her voice, although we could barely see her going down. We all just stood there, some thought it funny, and others were frightened. It looked like she would be killed. Mae was a sweet friend; she had to be alright. So we soon started pulling her out of that awful predicament. She didn't even look like a human being. She was wet with watermelon juice and red dirt from head to toe. No one could ever believe how bad she looked, not to have even been hurt. Now, if you have never believed in miracles you can believe this one. God really sent an angel to take care of Mae. But she was a sight to behold! I was a witness. We didn't get to eat watermelon that day, but we could rejoice we still had Mae!

My dad had to eventually stop farming because no one was left at home to help him. After my dad stopped farming, he became pretty miserable just sitting around the house all day. One day he told mom that he believed he would try to find a public job. He talked to a lot of people who had jobs, so he decided he would put in his application with West Point Manufacturing Company. So he did, and they gave him a job. He worked for them fifteen years, and he only missed working about three or four days. What a record! He said the day he walked out of that mill knowing that he'd never go back was one of the saddest days of his life. He made a lot of friends. His personality was one of a kind. While working he saved enough money to build a new house. They were so proud of that house.

Mama always planted a big garden. She canned vegetables for the winter, and they heeled sweet potatoes. One thing papa didn't do was to keep neither a cow nor hog. He said they would be too hard to have where they lived. One day papa was just sitting in his big chair as usual. A lady and a young son knocked on the door, and she asked if she could use the telephone, saying they were broken down and they needed help. Papa said, "Sure." Then he put his head back down.

The lady said, "Mr. Adams, you are sick, aren't you?"

Papa said, "Yes." She asked him if she could pray for him, and Papa said, "Please do." She laid one hand on his head and prayed; not only did his headache stop but for as long as I can remember he never had the headache again. Praise God!

After my dad retired from West Point Manufacturing Company, he just didn't have anything to do. He tried taking some walks everyday, and that got boring so he stopped. He tried to stop smoking, and did for eight months, but that didn't work. I could see a kind of sickness in his face. We tried to take him places, but to be honest he just wasn't interested in anything. He did get sick, and he asked me to take him to the doctor. I did, and he was put in the hospital. He stayed in the hospital three weeks. Floyd stayed every night, and I stayed every day. It was breaking my heart to see him failing so. On July 8, 1971, he passed away; our family chain had been broken. We all were so sad; it left Mama alone, but we kept someone living with her as long as she lived, which was ten more years. I miss them still, but I have good memories.

# A Tribute to Papa

**My Loving Dad**

It has been many years since my dad left us to go to be with Jesus. He has crossed over to the other side of life – where there is no sickness, no sorrow, nor tears – where there is all peace and joy. We didn't call him Dad; to us he was Papa. There were five in our family – one sister, one brother, Mama, Papa, and me.

I remember how tenderhearted and loving Papa was. And I'll never forget some of the things he taught us. He taught us the meaning of "love" and "respect." He said we should love everyone because Jesus first loves us. We were disciplined by our parents, and we respected them and loved them dearly. Papa believed in the old Proverb 22:6: "Train up a child in the way he should go; and when he is old, he will not depart from it."

I saw Papa read the Bible, and he would talk about what the Word says. He would tell us that only God can do all things – that He works through us to do the things on earth for His Glory. Papa would talk about not tempting God. He knew temptation was of Satan. I heard him say many times, "God sends rain on the just and on the unjust" – meaning that God is no respecter of persons.

Mama was Papa's helpmate; although their personalities were as different as day and night, they walked hand in hand. Mama was very quiet while Papa was a big talker, always making friends and never meeting a stranger. He played the banjo – had rhythm and could buck dance like a pro. He was lots of fun. He respected and was proud of his name. He told us that he met a man once who had his exact name, Herbert Holston Adams. This was very unusual. This man was a salesman of fountain pens. And he gave my dad one because they had the same name. Oh, I miss my dad so very much – only Jesus knows. There is a vacant place in my heart that can only be filled with the memories of him. I can still hear him talking as if it was only yesterday.

Papa didn't have a chance to get a good education, but he was very intelligent. He had the mind of "just knowing," an excellent memory, a wit as quick as lightning, and a smile that would give away his thoughts. Often I catch myself thinking about my childhood days. They were happy because there was a closeness among our family that's difficult to explain. We shared and communicated with each other. Our home was full of fun, laughter and play. That isn't to say that my sister, brother, and I always got along. We had our squabbles, but usually things would go back to normal really soon – with love.

My dad farmed, and his body was a perfect example of his work. He was tall in stature with long strong arms. His hands were large and calloused from holding on to that old plow day after day. He had a tan from the sun and lines of wisdom ran across his brow. He knew how to cultivate his farmland and just the right time to plant.

Even though we moved a lot, we always found good neighbors and friends wherever we lived. And even in difficult situations Papa managed to make a good honest living. While I was still very small, too young to really work, I always wanted to help my dad no matter what he did. Although he worked very hard, he always had time for us kids. He taught me to play the banjo, and I tried to dance as he did.

Many times I'd go to the field where Papa was plowing to take him a cool drink of water. I'd run across the freshly plowed ground and can almost feel the soft dirt beneath my bare feet even now. Sometimes he would sit down to rest for a little while, and we would just talk, maybe about needing a rain or maybe about himself growing up on the farm with his eleven brothers and sisters. He always had "interesting and funny" things to tell about the happenings of his growing up home life.

While sitting there, he'd take off his hat to cool his head; and I could see big drops of sweat running down his face. Oh, how I hated to see my dad so hot and tired. Soon he would look toward the sun whose warmth and shining rays gleamed like gold, and he would say, "I'd better get started back if I intend to finish this spot before sundown." We really didn't need a clock to tell the time; my dad worked from "sunup to sundown."

He would start his plowing again. Then I would play around, building a frog house or catching grasshoppers. Grasshopper catching was part of the childhood fun. I'm sure most people think grasshoppers are really ugly little creatures, but through the eyes of a child, I saw beauty. Some of them had wings that were as pretty and colorful as a Japanese fan. Some had beautiful blue behind their two long hind legs. They were my favorites. And there was one thing for sure – if one of those ever crossed my path I would catch him or run a mile trying. He might as well compromise.

I remember so well whether playing or working, it was dangerous for a grasshopper to come along because off came my bonnet and after him I would go. And it was a long time before I gave up my grasshopper catching. Sometimes I'd catch two or three and take them home with me and build a little rock house to put them in and get some green blades of grass and watch them eat like crazy. It was fun to see how fast they could nibble up that grass. The little story about "The Ant and The Grasshopper" always fascinated me.

The sun would soon start going down slowly over the horizon, and it would be time for Papa to stop his day's work and for us to go home. And since I had waited, I knew I'd get to ride the ole mule home. Anyone who has never ridden a mule bareback doesn't know what they have missed. Anyway, the ole mule didn't always agree to let me ride him. Once I remember when papa set me on his back, and he threw me off. But afterwards that old mule really got a whipping. Later, I wondered if a dumb mule could know what on earth he had done.

Anyway, I'd be so happy when we all sat around the table for our night's meal – we called it supper. Each of us had our own special place to sit. If one was missing it just wasn't the same. There was an empty feeling among the rest of the family. I remember once when a little friend wanted me to go spend the night with her; my sister cried and begged me not to go. And so it was with each of us – we hated to be separated.

All through my growing up years, I dreaded the fact to know as time and years go by all things must change. But years did not change my dad's views on life. His words were his actions and his actions were his proven words – even his silence was a language that was all his own and which was highly respected.

The year my little brother was born, I was eight. It was at this time I became a constant little worker in the field. But it wasn't too bad because I was a pretty big "tomboy" anyway. As one might say, "I was my dad's shadow." I watched him do all sorts of jobs that need to be done on a farm. And I tried to help him, whatever he did. He was always encouraging – never complaining if my work wasn't the best. And as I think of it now, I'm sure he was glad to have just a "little" help. Sometimes I would follow in his footsteps as he plowed – going up and down every row. I was so dependable, predictable, and especially observant. I was a faithful little chap. That's what Papa called us kids – "chaps."

Remembering those long bygone days, I sometimes sit and picture myself as a child again. I guess as we become older, our memories become more precious. Yes, my childhood memories are with me still. That isn't to say that everything was always perfect – far from it. But country life was so refreshing. Yes, we worked, but we could also find lots of fun time. We were so young and so full of energy.

As I grew older, I realized our family would not always be together living in one house. But deep inside I knew our love would remain the same. I remembered Papa telling us there was a Higher Power watching over us, and He would help us through life if we were obedient to Him. Well, as I study God's Word it brings back to mind the things Papa taught us. He was right. Yes, there is a Higher Power; He's our Master, Lord, and Savior. And as I pray, I can truly thank the Lord that I had a Dad who gave me a good start in life – making God my source.

Papa always taught us the value of giving. He would say, "It's more blessed to give than to receive." I suppose that's why he never had a lot of anything – he gave it away. There is an old saying, and it really fit my dad, "he would give the shirt off his back." He never owned an automobile nor had the luxuries that most people enjoy. But he had the best gifts that life has to offer – love and compassion. He told us many times to keep the Golden Rule: "Do Unto Others As You Would Have Them Do Unto You."

# The Story Continues

When Grace was about two years old, Edna was expecting again. They had another beautiful baby girl, and they named her Peggy. They were living near Huguley, Alabama, at the time, but Lowell wanted to move back to LaFayette. He was convinced that he wanted to go into the restaurant business. It was a long time before he found what he wanted, and they had already given birth to another baby by this time. It was a boy they named William, but everyone called him Bill. Lowell was very proud to have a son. He was a healthy looking baby and

was so adorable. Despite suffering some breathing problems, Bill lived to be in his sixties before passing away a couple of years ago. His sister Grace had already passed away from lung cancer. They are both deeply missed by our family.

As Grace was growing up she looked like a model. She was very tall and pretty as a picture. She was married to Paul Easterling, a good looking man with a good personality. They had three beautiful daughters, Leslie, Van, and Debbie. They are very sweet and smart. All three are married and have a happy family.

Peggy is still living and pretty as ever. She married and had two beautiful daughters, Teresa and Alicia. Although their dad has passed away now, but both girls are married and doing well and both have jobs. They have their own sweet families.

Peggy is now married to a wonderful man, Ed Moore. He is very talented and has a good voice for singing. He takes care of his family well. His personality is one of a kind. He and Peggy are church people, and they sing beautifully together!

Lowell eventually found this small café outside the city of LaFayette. He seized on the opportunity and was making decent money until the military drafted him into service for World War II. It was so sad to see him leave Edna and the little ones behind. Edna and the kids then were forced to move back in the house with our parents while Lowell was at war. Lowell was put on the front line to fight, and one day Edna received a telegram that Lowell had been killed. This was devastating news and a loss of such a great husband and dad.

Edna stayed sad for a very long time. We all tried to help her, but her world was torn apart. Later she met a good looking guy, Claude Jackson. They dated awhile, fell in love and got married. After their son Jimmy was born, they were very happy. Jimmy was a darling baby, and we all loved him. Claude, Edna's second husband, got sick and had to be put in the hospital. He didn't live long; he passed away leaving Edna and their small son, Jimmy. Papa said, "Now we must help them." Jimmy was too young to work. We all did what we could.

Jimmy missed his dad very much. He stayed close beside his mother while he was in school. After graduating he started looking for a job. He soon found a good job with the City of LaFayette. He was promoted several times, and he is still with the city today. He married Tammy Gooden at a young age, they had one son, and they named him James Lanier. They soon went their separate ways, and not so long after their separation Jimmy met Robin Padgett, a very beautiful young girl, and they got married. They have a beautiful daughter, Jimmy Lyn. She is very sweet and smart.

I thought maybe if Edna and I had a hobby, it would help her get her mind off Claude's death. I knew she used to like to fish; maybe we could start again. Mr. Darcy Tatum had a nice big lake, and he had told us we could go to his lake anytime and fish. So one day I told Edna to let's go fishing. She seemed eager to go. When we first got to the lake I said, "Edna, let us try fishing from the dam first." She said, "Ok." We were fishing with rods and reels. Real soon I hung a fish, but I wondered how I was going to bring him in since it was a long way from the top of the dam to the water. I said to Edna, "Let's think of a way that I can get down this dam."

Soon we rigged up a way. Edna was going to stand on the dam and hold one of my hands and my rod that had the fish and then I was going to slip and slide down the side of the big dam. Going down I would try to find a little bush to hold to, then reach down into the deep water to bring out the fish; big or little, I had hung a fish. We got so twisted and crossed up we looked like we were getting ready to do a circus act. It was a sight to behold! The fish was so small it almost looked like a tadpole.

I told Edna to lets move around to the other side of the lake, so we did. And just at that moment I saw a man in white overalls coming toward us. I said, "Oh, Edna, here comes the game warden, and we don't have any license." No sooner had I said that, then I saw our dad coming, then Mama. I said to Edna, "What has happened, I wonder?"

As the man walked up, he said, "Have you caught anything?" We learned that he wasn't a game warden; he was

Papa's next-door neighbor. He said, "I was expecting to find two little girls over here fishing. Your dad came over to my house and asked me if I would bring him over here to the lake. He said, "My chaps have gone fishing and haven't come home."

I said, "Yes, he has called us chaps since we were born." We all got a big laugh. Papa and mama loved us dearly. We started fishing a lot more. Many years later, my son, Darryl, wanted me to go fishing with him. I did, and we went back to Mr. Tatum's lake. That time I hung a fish so large I had to call to Darryl for help. When he reached me, he held my rod and tried to reel him in but could not. I waded out into the water, because at first I though my hook was hung on a root, but when I reached my hook I had a big fish on it. I reached down and pulled him up, and it was an eight-pound bass! We were so thrilled as we left to take our fish home. It will always be an unforgettable memory! Fishing to me is an enjoyable sport.

All through the years I can still remember my earliest childhood, even when I first started to school. The first school I attended was a two room building called the Red Hill School House. We had to walk nearly a mile to reach Red Hill, and we carried our lunch in a little brown paper bag. The winter days were bitter cold, and so many times the ground would be covered with ice. When we arrived to school, we only had one large wood heater to warm the entire space. We really didn't stay too warm the entire day! My sister was so sweet and protective of me; she would take off her coat and put it around me when we went home in the evenings. Our feet would even be frozen, and mine would often chap.

When I was promoted from Red Hill, I went to a new and larger school called Union Hill. Gone were the days of walking to school because now we could ride the school bus. We really thought we had it made, but it wasn't so long until there was a shortage of money for schools during the depression, so many

Thelma's Sixth Grade Class - March 25, 1930

schools closed. Soon a few private schools started, and my parents had moved from the country in Beat Four to a small community below LaFayette. At this time I was boarding and still going to Union Hill. I had made a lot of school friends. Many of the teachers thought I was very smart, and I remember how Mr. Eugene Causey bragged on my penmanship. He said that I could write better than anyone he had ever known. He always asked me to write the tests on the chalkboard, and he also had me to write his name on all the report cards – I thought that was pretty special. He was a very tall man, clean cut, very friendly, well liked, and a very good math teacher. I'll always remember him as a good friend and a wonderful teacher.

As I started writing the story of the ole school days at Union Hill, the very secret thought came to me about Mr. Causey. He was a wonderful teacher, and he knew math forward and backward. He made us students feel good about ourselves. Mr. Causey quite often wore a black bow tie to school and I can see him now standing tall at his desk, arms folded, looking over the room. During a study hall sometimes, he would give us a chance to tell something funny. He made school more enjoyable and taught us to help one another with a problem.

One day he asked me if I would put a test on the chalk board for the next student class. I said, "Okay, sure, I'll be glad to." The rest of the class left for study hall before I finished. After I finished I turned to go up to his desk to give him the test copy. He was standing tall at his desk, arms folded. He took one step towards me, he grabbed me so tight and kissed me so hard until I saw stars. I pulled away and ran as fast as I could to the study hall. Every head turned to look at me, and I heard someone say, "What's wrong with her?" The study hall teacher came to me and said, just sit right here and everybody kept quiet. I kept thinking about that black bow tie, and at that moment it flew across my heart, I must always keep this a secret. Although it never happened again, I believe he knew he frightened me. Time changes a lot of things, even keeping secrets. It has been approximately 79 years ago, and this is my first telling. Now you know!

I was elected to play on the basketball team and played the forward position. Mary McClendon was our basketball coach, and I loved to play and received many compliments. One of the other teachers who thought I was very smart was Mr. Dugen Denny. He told me that I was one of the best students he ever had. He was a great teacher and enjoyed his job. He was good to his students and always taught with a smile. After retirement from teaching school, he was elected as the tax assessor for the county, and he wanted me to be his secretary. He even asked my husband, Jimmy, if I could. Jimmy said no and that I had a job enough at home. Our first baby, Edwina, was only eight months old at the time. My mother had already told me she would keep the baby to allow me to be able to work, but the answer was still no because Jimmy never wanted me to be away from home and the kids. Mr. Denny was a nice looking guy and had a very friendly personality. I have many memories of my school days and can honestly say I truly enjoyed school.

My sister Edna didn't share the same sentiment towards attending school. She went one day in the twelfth grade and came home and told papa that she wasn't going back another day – and she never did. Union Hill eventually had to close, so I left and came back home. I started to the big city school in LaFayette and graduated there in 1936. Now I began thinking what the future might hold for me, and I knew exactly who held the future

– God. My dad was still farming after I graduated, and I said to him, "I would just wait and see what door God would open for me."

After I graduated from high school, I had big plans and wanted to become a cosmetologist. I sent off applications and already had my mind made up and bags packed. I heard from a beauty shop in Florida, and it sounded like a good opportunity. They wrote back and wanted me to describe myself to them so they could meet me at the bus station. They wanted to know what color dress I would be wearing so they could identify me when I arrived.

I had learned to finger wave hair and roll hair on brown paper. While attending school all the teachers would let me out Friday at noon to finger wave all the teachers' hair for the weekend and any neighbor close to school could also come. I had a friend that helped me some, and her name was Mae Lambert. Despite the interest from the beauty shop, I soon changed my mind because I just couldn't bring myself to leave my family and home behind. I put my trust in God and then waited to see what door He would open next.

One of the most difficult chapters in my life was when I began to realize that I was too old to play with dolls and too young to date. We lived in a good community with a lot of different age teenagers. We always planned parties and things that everybody could participate in, although most of the time the youngest stayed home. Sometimes my dad would play the banjo, and we would dance. If we wanted some games to do we'd build a seesaw, whirligig, or go snipe hunting. We had fun whatever we did. Everybody looked forward to coming to our house.

I guess I was the little silly one. I was always telling funny tales just to make everybody laugh. We had one guy to always show up whether invited or not. He drove a Model-T Ford, was good looking, and had a good personality. He seemed to have fun at our get togethers. One night we were all together and in rolled this boy. He wanted to see what we were doing. And silly me, I took the floor. I told about this cousin of mine, Cathleen Adams, coming to stay a few days with me. I told them we tried to find a lot of fun things to do. I told her one day to lets go down to the sweet gum tree and get us some sweet gum; that suited her, so we did. After getting a big chew, I said "I'm going to make me some specs." That's what old folks called eye glasses. She said I'll make me some too. We had fun chewing our sweetgum, and then we patted out little pieces and put them over our eyes.

In a short time I said, "I'm going to take mine off." She said, "I'm not, I'm going to wear mine to the house so hold my hand and lead me. I bet Aunt Lee will think I look like an outer space person." We went in the house and my mom said, "My goodness child, you better get that off your face before it won't come off." That scared her, and she started trying to pull it off. It had melted some to her face, and it would not come off. My mom put a little turpentine on it and some got in her eyes, and she started crying so loud. Now we lived far out in the country – no car, no doctor. But little by little mama started peeling off small pieces, and it seemed to be coming off. Mama said the wetness of the tears may have helped. Anyway, once it was off we were so glad, but her eyes were slightly swollen and red. A great lesson learned. Well it was time for Cathleen to go home, but we would always remember the sweetgum tree.

So many times we lived close by a creek; this time we lived near Hootalocco Creek. We could always find good fishing spots. Once Granny Adams came to spend a few days with us. We told her every time it rained the creek got muddy and the catfish would bite like crazy. She said, "I sure hope it rains, cause I sure like to fish." It did, so we gathered up our fishing gear and headed to the creek. The creek was so muddy and the fish were biting as fast as we could throw our hooks in. Granny and my sister Edna wanted me to stop fishing and string up the ones they had thrown on the bank. I thought I would tell a little joke, and maybe they would stop pitching fish out for me to string up.

So, I said "Hey y'all, I just saw a little mermaid; she was so cute. She gave three flips and went back into the deep water."

They said, "You're crazy! It's fixing to start getting dark; we've got to pick up the rest of the fish and go home." We counted our fish, and to the best of my knowledge we had caught ninety-seven – I kid you not! We picked up the rest of our stuff and headed home.

As we walked along, Granny jumped and said, "Watch out!"

I said, "What is it, Granny?"

She said, "A snake," and I said, "Let's run!"

She said, "Oh no, he said he was going down to the creek and look for that little mermaid."

I said, "Ah, Granny!" She knew she had turned the joke on me, and she laughed all the way to the house.

The day Granny went home Mr. Allen came to see my dad. He said he just wanted to talk to him. He told papa that the boy with the Model-T Ford was driving too fast through the neighborhood, and he was stealing. Papa asked what had he stole, and Mr. Allen told him chickens. My dad said, "My, my, Mr. Allen."

Mr. Allen said, "Yes, he was walking to the country store the other day, and he was passing Mr. Scott's house, and he started running after one of Mr. Scott's chickens. Mr. Scott heard the chickens; they sounded like something was after them." Sure enough there was a guy after one of Mr. Scott's chickens.

Mr. Scott hollered, "Hey son, what's wrong?"

The guy said, "I was carrying my chicken to the store, and he got away from me." There was a country store in our community, and it was not too far to walk.

Mr. Scott said, "Wait, I will help you catch him." Mr. Scott hemmed up his big rooster, handed it to the guy and said, "Here son, hold him right and don't let him get away again."

The boy said, "Thank you!" and away he went.

Mr. Scott said he stood there scratching his head, saying to himself, "I do believe that was my chicken I just gave away!" In fact, it was Mr. Scott's chicken, and he had been hoodwinked.

Mr. Scott watched his chicken out of sight. He picked himself up off the ground and wiped the tears from his eyes and made a promise to himself, "When in doubt, don't!"

Mr. Allen said, "Mr. Adams, we must try to get rid of that rascal."

Late that afternoon the boy came to our house. No sooner had he walked in than my dad came to the door and said, "Thelma, it's bed time." Now we all know that folks don't go to bed before dark. I was so embarrassed. It had been two years since I had met this boy; we had grown to care more for one another. My mom was in the kitchen, and she called me to come there. I went to see what she wanted.

She said, "Thelma, you known how much I love you, and I don't want to see you hurt. I had rather follow you to your grave than to see you marry that boy." Yes, I was sad awhile, but the more I thought about what the Bible says, the better I felt. In Ephesians 2:3 it says, "Honour thy father and mother, that it may be well with thee, and thou mayest live long on the earth." I wasn't that little girl anymore. I had grown up, and I knew right from wrong. I was getting my school behind me and waiting for that special someone. God has taught me. He has been my guide for ninety-six years. He is my loving God.

One night, to my surprise, two boys and a girlfriend of mine, Aileene Henderson, came to our house and wanted me to go with them to her house. She said that they were having a weenie roast in their pasture and there were more boys attending than girls. I had already gone to bed, so I told her I wouldn't be able to go with them. Then I asked her who were the boys with her, and she said, "James Eason and James Rodgers."

I said, "Well I know James Eason; he's alright, but I don't want to date him. What about this James Rodgers?"

She said, "He's new here. He came from South Alabama to work for his brother, J.D., sawmilling." At first I thought to myself that this didn't sound too promising. Then she said, "Honey, jump up and get dressed and let's go; we're not going to marry them anyway!"

Well, since she kept insisting, I got up, dressed, and went with them to the weenie roast. To my surprise I had a good time, and I met a lot of people since many came from town. We had

not been living in that community long, but everyone seemed extremely joyful. It was a good way to get acquainted with new people if nothing else. After that night, James "Jimmy" Rodgers started writing little notes asking me for dates. We soon started going together steady, and he was so nice and a perfect gentleman. We had lots of common passions, and I thought he was very good looking. He began telling me how hard he had worked to make enough money to come to LaFayette. His brother, J.D., owned a large saw mill and logging outfit along with other businesses, and he told Jimmy he would give him a job. Times were hard, and Jimmy thought the offer sounded good so he decided to try it out and get some money while he could.

He said he started out doing work in the fields for whomever would hire him. He needed a car and some gas money, and he said he worked hard for thirty-five cents a day. Slowly but surely he made enough to accomplish those goals. He bought a 1928 Ford Model A Roadster with a rumble seat; he gave

seventy-five dollars for it and still had enough money to put some gas in the tank.

He then thought it was time to say goodbye to his old friends and hello to new ones he would meet when he reached his destiny in LaFayette. He said he left a girlfriend that he liked, but he was looking forward to having a better job. He thought if he didn't like the place he was moving, he could always go back home. He owned forty acres of land close to Andalusia, Alabama, but later sold it, so that let me know he never intended to go back down to South Alabama to live.

Well so it happened, Aileene married James Eason, and, of course, I married James Rodgers, whom I started calling Jimmy the night we met at the weenie roast. Never in a million years did I think I would marry him. We dated for one year and got married September 16, 1939. That has been over seventy-four years ago, and we are still very much in love. I am ninety-six years old and he is ninety-nine. Love has no end!

It was at this time that we were living in United States Senator Tom Heflin's house. In fact, Tom Heflin, his sister and her husband, Mr. and Mrs. Reeves, were living there, too. They lived upstairs, and we lived in the big downstairs. We got very acquainted with all of them. They were all very friendly with us. Mr. Heflin still wore his long frock tail coat, hot or cold. He was a perfect gentleman. When he would walk to the restaurant, Jimmy would take him home. When Mr. Heflin passed away, Jimmy was one of the Pallbearers.

I talked with Mrs. Reeves many times; she knew how sick my son Darryl was. But she told me to be careful how I prayed. She said she knew this lady that wanted a baby so bad until she asked God to just let her have a baby, nothing else mattered. She said that mother had a baby, and she lived to see him hanged. What a tragic story! She said just ask God if it be His will. She was a sweet lady, and we learned to love them.

As the years went by I still think about how happy we all were when Floyd came home from the World War II. He had been blessed so many times. When he was first drafted in World War II service, they put him in the 42$^{nd}$ Infantry Rainbow Division as a medic. He was never directly in the front-line fighting, but it was very sad to him to help take care of the wounded and to liberate our captured soldiers. When he came home our dad was still farming, and Floyd stayed home for a while before getting a public-sector job.

Floyd later met a beautiful girl by the name of Myrtle Cline. They dated for awhile and were soon married. They were very much in love, and our entire family loved her and her sweet disposition. She was like a sister to both Edna and me. Floyd and Myrtle each had jobs and soon started their own family. They had two beautiful little girls. The oldest one is Sonya, who is now married with two children. The youngest girl is Cheryl, who is also married and has four children of her own. All is well with them, and they are a very happy family. Unfortunately, their parents have passed away, and I still miss them very much.

Sonya Adams

When I start thinking over the ninety-six years of my life, I start with today – I have seen good days and bad days, but the good always outweighs the bad. We must remember prayer availeth much. We have a good prayer life today, and we serve an awesome God. My mother was so sweet when she started telling us about Jesus while we were very young. She taught us the prayer, "Now I lay me down to sleep" and others. I would ask her day after day, "Mama, if I start right now being good, will I go to Heaven?" She would always say, "Yes."

Sometimes I think back about when Jimmy and I first met. We only dated about a year before we got married, and he told me one day that he wanted to stop sawmilling and find another job. I was surprised when he told me he believed he would like to own a restaurant. There was a small service station up town that had been turned into a very small café and the man that was operating it wanted out. Sometime around 1940, Jimmy bought his restaurant equipment and started his new job, never thinking how many roads he would travel through the coming years. This place only had one long countertop with eight stools and was only equipped to serve sandwiches. When he started, Jimmy sold hamburgers, hot dogs, coffee, and more for only a nickel each. A T-bone steak was 75 cents!

People began to want vegetables, so Jimmy got busy and began enlarging the restaurant. First, he had a big dining room added on the front with all new furniture. It turned out to be a beautiful renovation, and business increased dramatically. He then added another large dining area in the back for parties, clubs, and meetings. Everything was looking great at that point, so he added another smaller room off to one side of the main dining room. We even had customers from surrounding towns coming to eat with us. He hired more waitresses and cooks and added a large kitchen with all new equipment. By this time the place did not look like a café, so we put a name in big lights on the outside – "Rodgers Restaurant."

Business kept growing, but in the Forties during World War II, we were given stamps to put with money to buy gas, and we were given tokens to put with the money to buy food. We were just allotted so much per family. I remember two things particularly that we were allotted to buy, meat and sugar. It was very rough on Jimmy with his being in the restaurant business, but he had a close friend that helped him out. His friend and his wife didn't need many groceries, so he would go shopping with Jimmy and get in the grocery line and buy the groceries Jimmy needed, and when they left the store he let Jimmy have them. He was a special friend and lifesaver for the restaurant.

About twenty years passed, and a man by the name of Luther Liles wanted to buy our restaurant in LaFayette. Jimmy thought about it for a while but finally agreed to sell it to him. Jimmy thought by now he knew everything about restaurants, and he said he would like to have a bigger one. We had heard that the Heart of Auburn was for sale. We went down to see it, and sure enough it was very nice and even joined with the hotel. After many discussions we decided to take the restaurant and give it a chance. At first, business was so busy that Jimmy hardly knew what to do to maintain this hectic pace. His main cook gave him a lot of insights and helped Jimmy catch on to things quickly. Everything went well, and business stayed excellent for a long time. Jimmy had some of the best cooks that he could have ever hoped for.

Through all the different restaurants we owned, we managed to keep good waitresses and cooks. There is one cook I could never forget, and her name was Anna Mae Webb. She worked for us for many, many years. She worked real hard, prepared great tasting food, and kept things so clean. Not only did she work in the restaurant, but she helped me with my house work, such as mopping,

washing windows, etc. Then we would go to the yard and dig a while, setting out azaleas or small trees and digging up grass where it didn't belong. She had a very sweet personality. She loved people and tried to get along with everyone.

She kept my kids when I needed her. I remember once when she was taking care of my son, Darryl. They were playing at the small playground that was behind the restaurant. She was letting him walk the "high bar" with his hands, and he fell and broke his little arm. When I got to him, he was crying and so was she; she was holding him in her arms.

Later, when Edwina, my daughter, was diagnosed with a brain tumor, Edwina called Anna from the ambulance going to Birmingham, because at the time she was very upset and she could only remember Anna's number. Anna told me later that she herself cried because she was so touched that her number was the only one Edwina could remember. Anna has passed away now, leaving her legacy as a helper and a good friend!

We stayed in business at the Heart of Auburn for four and a half years. The landlord kept increasing Jimmy's rent until he thought it wasn't worth it, so he started looking for another restaurant. He had made a lot of friends, and someone told him that the University Motor Lodge Restaurant was available for rent. That was uptown Auburn, so Jimmy went to investigate and agreed to go into business there. Jimmy got acquainted with the man that ran the hotel, Mr. Meadows, and they became the best of friends. Jimmy liked the University Motor Lodge, and he had a strong business, good cooks, and nice waitresses.

Everything was going well, but Luther Liles later decided he couldn't continue the payments for the restaurant, so we had to take it back from him. That meant we would have to leave the University Motor Lodge and return to LaFayette. We had been there four years, and it was a great place. We decided there was only one thing left for us to do, and that was to try to sell the restaurant in Auburn and take back our old restaurant and go from there.

We really didn't want our restaurant in LaFayette to stay closed, so we just gave up the University Motor Lodge and came back home in LaFayette. Jimmy had commuted for nearly ten years, and it was getting a little hard on him to continue to do so with gas increasing in price and ultimately contributing to more overhead expense. Besides, one night in March of 1970, when Jimmy was leaving Auburn to come home, it was storming, and a tree fell across the road and landed on his car. Another miracle – God protected him; the car was destroyed, but he was okay, even though his hat brim and coat were covered in broken glass. There were even pieces of glass in his pockets! Soon we had made everything alright in Auburn and came back home to LaFayette. We never sold our house in LaFayette even though someone wanted to buy it while he was in business in Auburn. We had lots of cleaning and buying that was necessary for us to open back up the old restaurant. We fixed it up again and stayed in business until Jimmy's retirement in 2007. In total, Jimmy was in the restaurant business for sixty-seven years. It was a very long journey but an enjoyable one.

During Jimmy's many years in the restaurant business, his goal was always to serve the public. He loved the people and appreciated their

## Letters to the Editor

Dear Editor:

Rodger's Restaurant, no one can remember when it wasn't there. We certainly can't. Occupying strategically a corner one block south of the courthouse forever classifies it as a historical landmark in our book.

To a lot of people, passing by on the way to fast food, it might seem an outdated, time consuming alternative to their pit stop, drive-thru plastic-ware meal experience. But let us enlighten you, there is a gracious old southern gentleman with a lifetime of experience behind that apron who will share a cup of coffee and catch you up on local current affairs as you enjoy the friendly atmosphere.

To anyone who doesn't know what we're talking about, somewhere mixed in with the hamburgers and fries, fried chicken, steaks and breakfast, is an ingredient that you can get hooked on. It has been added for over 50 years by Mr. Jimmy, it's called Southern Hospitality.

Thanks Mr. Jimmy!!
The Breakfast Club

support and patronage, and Jimmy was always willing to help. One Thanksgiving, Jimmy gave away dinners to anyone who said that they were unable to fix their own meal. If they were shut in and had no way to come and get it, we delivered it to them. He was always caring and giving.

During ice or snowstorms, especially when there was no electricity, he would get to the restaurant early and open. He would say that the city and T.R.E.C. workers would need a place to eat and get warm. Since he cooked with gas and had gas heat, people could come in and at least get a warm meal. I remember one time using kerosene lamps on the tables for light. Upon his retirement, the City Council declared Jimmy Rodgers Day and awarded him a certificate of recognition for his many years of helping and serving others through his business.

When Jimmy and I first married, I wanted to have a baby, but he was a little hesitant at first. However, after we were married for three years, I was expecting. We waited anxiously for the event and when the time came we had the most beautiful little girl. My sister said she was the prettiest newborn she ever saw. We named her Janice Edwina. Growing up she was always sweet spirited and had many wonderful talents. When she was in the first grade every teacher in the school stood in their doorway every morning just to see Edwina walk down the hall. I didn't know this until school was out that year, and one of the teachers told me. I made all of her little outfits and usually parted her hair in two pig tails – she was precious. When

she started in the third grade, she was chosen by all the teachers in LaFayette to be the 'Queen of Chambers County.' There was a big parade to be held in Columbus, Georgia, that was in honor of High Neighbor Day. Edwina was to ride on a big float with other little girls from their respective counties. I made her a beautiful little evening dress to wear for this float, and she looked so pretty. It was a great experience for her, and hundreds of people lined the streets to watch the parade.

Edwina regularly attended church and sang in the choir. She graduated from LaFayette High School and attended Auburn University for four years, completing her undergraduate studies as an English major. While attending Auburn she met the man of her dreams, Travis Collins, who was from the small farming community of Utica, Mississippi. They fell in love and were married on July 25, 1964. Edwina looked so beautiful walking down the church aisle. Pastor Clark of First Baptist Church in LaFayette married them, and many people were in attendance.

Edwina and her husband, Travis, lived in Auburn after they were married. Travis had received his undergraduate degree from Mississippi State University and had moved to Alabama to attend Veterinary School at Auburn University when he met Edwina. He eventually became one of the best veterinarians in the Southeast. While he was finishing his degree, Edwina taught English at Valley High School. After Travis became a veterinarian, he tried out two or more places to work but soon had a call to come to Atlanta, Georgia. Both were very excited and happy over the offer. Travis was good looking and had one of the best personalities. He was also a Colonel in the U.S. Army Reserve, 81$^{st}$ Airborne Division, a Special Forces Green Beret, and shot on the All Army Pistol Team  for almost thirteen years. He earned the prestigious Distinguished Pistol Shot award in 1975.

    Travis and Edwina lived in Atlanta together for over 30 years. During that time, I went up there often, and Edwina would come home to spend time with us. One time, when she came down, it was a heartbreaking experience. She and I were just sitting and watching television, and she jumped up and said, "Mother, something is happening to me." She had a light seizure, and we rushed her to the hospital. After the doctor ran a CAT scan, they told her they needed to send her to Birmingham to the University of Alabama Medical Center (UAB). After Birmingham and more tests, they told us that she had a tumor on her brain. After a biopsy surgery, they told us it was malignant and it could not be removed. Our hearts were broken, but she was so sweet through this whole ordeal. She stayed here in LaFayette with us to take radiation and other treatment.

My daughter, Edwina, lived with cancer of the brain for over seven years. She complained so little and loved all who came to see her. She lived her last years with her dad and me because her husband had already passed away with a heart attack on September 5, 2002. She passed away peacefully in 2009, but it still seemed like our world had ended. It was so sad for all of us.

*I looked upon*
*My beautiful daughter*
*And tears ran down my face –*
*Although I knew*
*That God had placed*
*A precious flower*
*In Heaven's vase!*

Before all of this happened with Edwina, they had a darling baby boy they named Jason Travis. He was so precious; not a blemish was on him, and he was such a joy. I had the opportunity to keep him regularly, and I know he loves me to this day. All during his childhood all he saw was mostly pavement, so when we kept him, he would want to ride on dirt roads. We did, and he enjoyed it so much. I even built him a swing in our big poplar tree, and we both had a great time swinging. We never had a dull moment when he was around.

When he was old enough, his parents sent him to kindergarten. It was held in a big church, a very wonderful, safe place. They had fine excellent teachers, and everything went well. When they graduated they wore little caps and gowns. The children looked so sweet in the commencement; they did so well!

Jason started to school, and he was a straight A student throughout school. He graduated and went into the antique and home furnishings business, but soon he was looking for something else. He still lives in Atlanta. He met a beautiful girl named Tonya Aumack, and they are now married. Jason works with technology and computers and Tonya is a librarian – she is so smart, and we all love her.

Going back to the story of Jimmy and me, after we had our first child, Edwina, I was soon expecting once again. On January 24, 1944, we had a darling little baby boy, and we named him Darryl Lee. He was the sweetest child I ever saw. He was

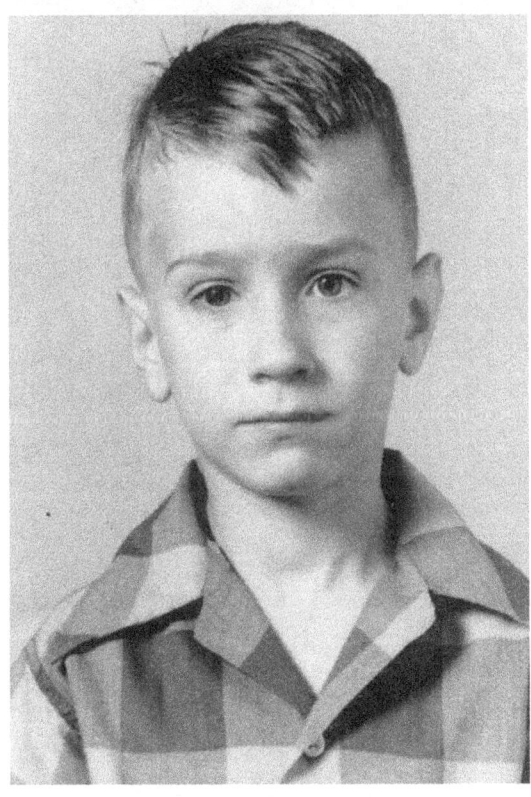

sick throughout his childhood. When he was very young, he had pneumonia three times. We soon found a good doctor in Atlanta, Georgia. He ran every test that could be run to try to find out what was wrong. When the doctor told me that he had asthma and his lungs were covered in dust, I was devastated and sad. He said it was up to me to help get him well. We lived close to a cotton gin, and I knew we had lots of dust, but I had never thought the cotton gin could have been making him sick. I had to sweep, mop, and dust every day. We moved from place to place until we got away from as much dust as possible. Unfortunately, he often stayed sick, and he couldn't play like the other kids. It hurt me badly when he'd say to me, "Mother, if I could breathe like you" – I often cried and prayed. I just couldn't stand to see my sweet baby so sick.

Darryl grew up and finished high school in LaFayette and went on to attend Auburn University, graduating with a Bachelor of Science degree. He taught high school until retirement, and we are so proud of him. He will always be a loving son. While Jimmy was at the University Motor Lodge Restaurant in Auburn, Darryl met a beautiful young girl by the name of Barbara Smith.

They began dating, fell in love and got married on March 20, 1970. She is a sweet wife and just about the best daughter-in-law one could ever hope for. She graduated from Auburn University in psychology, and she later obtained her Master's degree in education. Barbara taught school for 26 years before retiring from teaching. She then worked fifteen years at Marannook, a Christian youth camp near LaFayette, before retiring once again. She is so smart in many different ways, and we love her very much.

During the mid-seventies, our children, Edwina and Darryl, recorded a record together, along with singer/musician Anita Holm. The master tape was recorded in Atlanta, and the record was cut in New York. Shortly after, Travis, who was in the Army Reserve, had his annual two-week active duty in New York City. He and Edwina invited Darryl and Barbara to go with them. Because they were meeting the producers of their record, Darryl took his guitar with them.

While in New York, Travis volunteered Darryl to play his guitar and sing at the Army Reserve General's Ball. Edwina and Darryl also performed (played and sang) at the Top of the Gate and The Bitter End. They were invited back the next week, but time didn't allow them to return.

Long before the New York trip, Darryl and Edwina would practice singing together with Darryl playing the guitar. Both had beautiful voices, and they sounded so good together. Darryl was self-taught and played by ear.

We had many good singers and musicians that came to our house to practice together. Joel Williams was an excellent and talented piano player; he was one of the best. Razzy Bailey,

Hiram Love, and Claude Walton were all guitar players; they were really good. Edwina sang with the group on the Roanoke, Alabama, radio station. Razzy kept up his career and he reached the top of the charts with several hit songs. He is the best, and we are so proud of our hometown star. We count him as our own "country boy" from LaFayette, Alabama. I don't think any one will ever beat Razzy. We love him, and we try to follow his career and enjoy hearing about him.

Some other talented musicians and singers that Darryl often met with to "pick and grin" were Ralph Browning, a master guitarist, Ralph's sons, and Leroy Jones, singer and guitar player.

Darryl and Barbara learned they couldn't have children, but they didn't give up hope. They adopted a two month old little baby girl and named her Amanda Lee. She was so beautiful, and all the years she was growing up she really loved her mom and dad.  She went to Chambers Academy for two years and then three years at Springwood School in Lanett, both private schools. Her mom then home schooled her until she finished high school. She received a scholarship to Southern Union State Community College in Wadley, Alabama, where she was a member of the Show Choir and Southern Union Sound and Phi Theta Kappa. She graduated in 2008. By this time, she had met a wonderful young man at First Baptist Church in LaFayette, who became her husband. His name is Stephen Grubbs, and he's a good looking guy and has a great personality – you can tell they are very much in love. In fact, he graduated seminary in 2011 and is a Baptist minister. They have started their family, and they have the cutest little five year old son named Nathan, who is so loving and sweet. They also have a three year old little girl named Natalie, who's a doll, and a one year old son, Noah. We're so proud to be great-grandparents.

I have had many mishaps and surgeries. I broke my right foot several years ago getting out of a sport car that had the seat belt on the floor board. A few years later, I broke my right leg above my ankle really badly – I still have a steel plate connecting the bones. About three years later I fell out of the church door the night my granddaughter had her wedding rehearsal and broke my right hip. I was very sad that I didn't get to go to Amanda's wedding. Later on I was at home and fell and broke my left hip but have since recovered. I have had gallbladder, thyroid, and cataract surgeries. God has truly healed them all. I am seeing well, and I can walk without support. I am a walking miracle – praise God! I went to see my doctor not very long ago, and he looked at me and said, "Did you know that you would pass for seventy years old?" What a compliment!

In the nineteen-seventies and early nineteen-eighties there were so many prayer groups being organized. I was in one that Bibbie Tucker was leading. We met at her house more than any

other place. Later she got a trailer, and she fixed it up just for our meetings. Our group averaged in size between fifteen and twenty, more or less. Pat Carver, from Atlanta, Georgia, was our Bible Study Teacher. She has passed away now, but she left much of her excellent Bible studies with us. We will always remember her. Having these prayer meetings as we did allowed our faith to grow. But still something wasn't just right all the time. We had gone a little too far out on a limb. The more we studied the more we realized how to pray to get results; "If we ask anything according to His will, He heareth us: And if we know that He hears us, whatsoever we ask, we know that we have the petitions that we desired of Him," I John 5:14-15. I know we all know what the Bible says is the meaning of faith, but I also like Romans 4:17: "Calleth those things which be not as though they were." So, if we study the Bible, the Holy Spirit will guide us into God's will.

At this time it seemed that prayer groups were springing up everywhere. Going to these prayer groups and Bible studies really helped me to understand God's Word. But I must tell about an instance where we failed big time. When Edwina, my daughter, lived in Atlanta, I visited her quite often as I explained earlier. On this particular visit this prayer group was trying to figure out a place to have their meeting. Edwina had a wonderful friend named Ann Plampin; she was a real prayer warrior. They met at different places, so while discussing where to go someone said, "Let's go to that bank up town!" That suited everyone, so three or four car loads pulled out for the bank. I felt leery about it, but I was only a visitor. I wondered all the way there if the bank was in business, or had it closed? We arrived, and everyone

got out of their cars. Ann went straight for the doors. She called me, of all people, to come there. I did, and she said, "Thelma, lets both put our hands on the door knob and pray, and the door will open." All of a sudden she said, "Oh! I believe I felt the knob move, did you?" At that moment, I felt so foolish, and I believe she did as well. I just said keep praying, but I knew if that door opened, every police car in town would be after us, and we all would spend the night in jail. The bank was in business. It is good to have faith, but don't try to be foolish proving it!

I have heard that it is hard to find a true friend. Maybe so, but I feel that I have had one, and her name was Pearl Cain. I had been notified of a new couple in our church, but I had not met them.

Her husband was named Gene; he had been to college, and he was a good Bible scholar. They came over to our restaurant one Sunday to have lunch, and that's how I met Pearl. I learned that we had something in common. She had a married daughter living in Atlanta, and so did I. She asked me did I go to see my daughter very often. Jimmy spoke up and said, "Yes, I think she will finally move up there." We all had a big laugh. She said, "The next time you go to see your daughter, could I catch a ride and go see mine?" That's the way we were drawn closer together; we alternated trips. We shared a close friendship. We went shopping, ate out, and just had lots of fun. She has passed away now, and I sure have missed her. I feel that I have a lot more friends, and I enjoy their friendship and love all of them.

We are members of the First Baptist Church in LaFayette, Alabama. We still live in the house that we had built in the early sixties. We try to practice, "Do unto others as you would have them do unto you." Our pastor is Reverend Bill Hand, and we are so blessed to have him. He is so good, with a wonderful personality. He has a sweet, friendly wife, Laura, and three beautiful daughters, Alison, Emily, and Amy. They are all very sweet. Bill and Laura have their first grandchildren, Jackson, now a precious three  year old little boy, and his sister, Zoe, just turned one.

As part of the Bicentennial celebration of the United States, in July of 1976, our church commemorated this important event by members dressing in the fashions of 1776. I went to Atlanta and bought a long cotton dress that was real pretty. We all thought it looked like what Martha Washington would wear. My daughter found a wig that was styled in the same way as the colonial period. We got busy and found some blue material that matched my dress and my daughter-in-law, Barbara, made Jimmy the most eloquent outfit for the colonial period – his pants were knee breaches with buckles and his coat was a long frock tail. I sewed ruffles around his sleeves and made him a ruffled dickey to wear under the coat. Again, my daughter found her dad a white wig in the colonial fashion. I cut out big gold buckles for his shoes. He wore old gold rimmed frames with no lenses. When we both dressed, we looked so much like George and

Martha Washington that many people thought that's who we were! During our celebration and program at church, the other members did not even recognize Jimmy! 'George Washington' was a church usher that day!

At the urging and insistence of a friend, Jimmy wore his George Washington outfit to Auburn one day and was such a hit that he made the front page of <u>The Auburn Plainsman</u>, Auburn University's newspaper, July 22, 1976.

No, it is not George Washington. No, he is not running for mayor. He simply came to Auburn for a haircut. Jimmy Rogers, a resident of nearby Lafayette, shocked downtown shoppers Tuesday as he appeared in his colonial garb. It would have made a great campaign stunt though, wouldn't it?

Photo by Wanda Kenton

What a tragedy! Soon after I had finished writing the last chapter of my life I was in a bad car wreck. Jimmy and I went down to Auburn one afternoon to pick up my new eye glasses at Auburn Eye Care. We started to leave – we got in the car, buckled up, and started backing out to come home. The car started going in reverse real fast. I started screaming for Jimmy to put on the brakes. The harder he tried the faster the car went. We were now crossing five lanes of the Auburn-Opelika Road. But I know now why no car came through those lanes – God was

standing in the mist of those lanes with his arms stretched forth. They are usually heavy with traffic. Our car just got faster and faster until we ran in a ditch and hit a tree. It was a terrible hit. When the seat belt tightened around me, I really thought I was dying. I did not know when they took me out of the car that it was totaled. The car was a red Buick Park Avenue. Looking back, we believe the accelerator stuck.

I stayed in the hospital and rehab several weeks. Jimmy was not hurt, but he was very shook up. We just praised the Lord for his mercy. After I was out of the hospital for about two weeks, Jimmy got sick and had to go to see the doctor. They put him in the hospital immediately with double pneumonia; he was so very sick. He fought to live for three days while he was at Lanier Hospital in Valley, Alabama, and at one point his heart stopped, and they had to revive him. They soon moved him to East Alabama Medical Center (EAMC) in Opelika, AL. By the next day he was breathing on his own and looked much better. We had been standing around his bed and our heats were just breaking. Much prayer went up for him. The doctors came in and asked if we wanted to ask any questions. I asked Dr. Williams (his heart doctor) if he had any hope of recovery. He said "Well, he has about a 50/50 chance." As we left the room we felt more optimistic because Jimmy looked better, and we know that prayer is a stepping stone to healing.

  The beauty of the car accident is that so many people have said it was a miracle. Praise the Lord there are those who still believe in miracles. It truly was. A lot of people could have been hurt, but I was the only one and God has already healed me. What a mighty God we serve, a mighty King and a wonderful Savior!

*When I reach that mountain top*
*My journey will just begin*
*I will look up toward Heaven*
*For Heaven has no end!*

*July 2012*

My husband and I feel so blessed in unaccountable ways. We feel that God has added extra days to our lives as he did for Hezekiah in the Bible. God added fifteen extra years to his life and I know he has to ours. Jimmy is now ninety-nine years old, and I am ninety-six, as I write this little story of my life. We have celebrated our seventy-fourth wedding anniversary.

The narrative that's related in my chapters of this little book is about some of the highlights of my journey for these past ninety-six years. This journey will walk one through the pages of how I have been blessed beyond measure. I have also had some frightening experiences in my life. I was once given three minutes to live, and I remember seeing the edge of Jesus' head facing me. I only said, "Jesus, heal me," and He did. I can still see that vision today. God is a miracle working God! I don't know if I spoke in the natural or in the spirit; God knows, it was real! I know with this near death experience that God has blessed me time after time. This is how I met my doctor, Dr. Mitchel Galishoff. That was many years ago, and he is still my doctor today. He is a kind, sweet, Christian person. With God's help and power, he saved my life; I love him for being my doctor. May God always bless him.

I am in awe that the Lord has blessed me with over nine and a half decades of life – almost a century! Young people today cannot imagine how people once lived, but I believe they were happier then than most are today. They lived simply and happily, used what they had, and never thought one day a man would walk on the moon! We took our baths in a washtub in the kitchen; the well water was heated on the wood-burning stove. Now, not only is there indoor plumbing, there are fancy whirlpool tubs and showers that massage you while you bathe. We had to go outside to an "outhouse" to take care of business. Now there are toilets that flush themselves. We cleaned our clothes by boiling them in an open wash pot over a wood-burning fire. Later, we used a washboard and a galvanized tub. Finally, there was the old wringer washer that agitated the clothes, but to wring them out, you had to put them through the wringer that squeezed out the water. You were really in trouble if your hand or arm got caught in that wringer! Today, washers and dryers are programmable, and you can set them for clothing type, temperature, spin speed, etc. My, we've come a long way.

As I said earlier, my dad only had a horse and wagon for transportation. Today there are cars that tell you when there is a problem and how to get to where you're going.

When I was a young girl, penmanship (handwriting) was very important and good penmanship was greatly admired. Today, few write on paper any more; they just type on their computer. I remember using an old crank phone that hung on the wall. You had to go through an operator for all your calls. Now there are "smart phones" that are way too smart for me! I don't even know all the things they can do.

I remember Uncle Roscoe having an RCA Victrola. We listened to records on phonograph players. Today music is digital, whatever that means! I remember going to the movie theater to see black and white silent movies. Now, movies are not only in color, they are HD and 3D! Our first television was a black and white screen, and we were able to get three different channels, if we were lucky! Today we have a flat screen HDTV that gives me all kind of information about what I am watching, with more channels than I can use, if I can only figure out how to use the remote control!

In my lifetime, I have been blessed to see a lot of changes and a whirlwind of new inventions that as a child were unimaginable.

I have lived to write these chapters of my life with the help of my precious grandson Jason, who is very sweet and so smart. I started writing poems in my late seventies, and Jason said he would arrange everything for my autobiography and all of my poems in a book. My wonderful son, Darryl, and his wife, Barbara, have been an inspiration for encouraging me to do this. My lovely daughter always wanted me to put my poems in a book. She was my very special helper, and I miss her still. Last but not least, my husband, who has always been my love and a joy to be with – he is so special. I thank each one of those around me so much for their inspiration and support. My family has always been my joy, and I love them more than words can express!

*I am excited!*
*My love,*
*Hope you find some joy, fun, and be*
*blessed!*
*As Jimmy and I grow older,*
*We walk more slowly,*
*Holding hands along the way.*
*We'll soon be climbing those*
*Golden Stairs*
*To meet our Savior*
*Face to face –*
*For we have won*
*Our long awesome race!*

"Live a good life, it's not the years in a life but it's the life in the years."
- Abraham Lincoln

Thelma & Laura Lee Childers at Age 16 or 17

Thelma Standing on Porch of Present Home - 1960's

### ADAMS-RODGERS

The marriage of Miss Thelma Adams, daughter of Mr. and Mrs. H. H. Adams, to James Edward Rodgers of LaFayette, formerly of Andalusia, Ala., was solemnized last Saturday morning, September 16, at 11:30 o'clock. Judge Grady officiated in the presence of a few close friends.

The bride was lovely in a costume of navy blue triple crepe with matching accessories. She wore a corsage of sweetheart and tube roses, which added a touch of beauty. She is a graduate of LaFayette High School and active in social affairs.

The groom is the so nof S. N. Rodgers of Andalusia. He received his education at Red Levil High School and for the past two years has been engaged in business in LaFayette.

Immediately after the ceremony the couple left for a motor trip through South Alabama and points of interest in Florida. Congratulations.

Jimmy & Thelma in New York City - April 1974

Jimmy & Thelma's 70$^{th}$ Wedding Anniversary

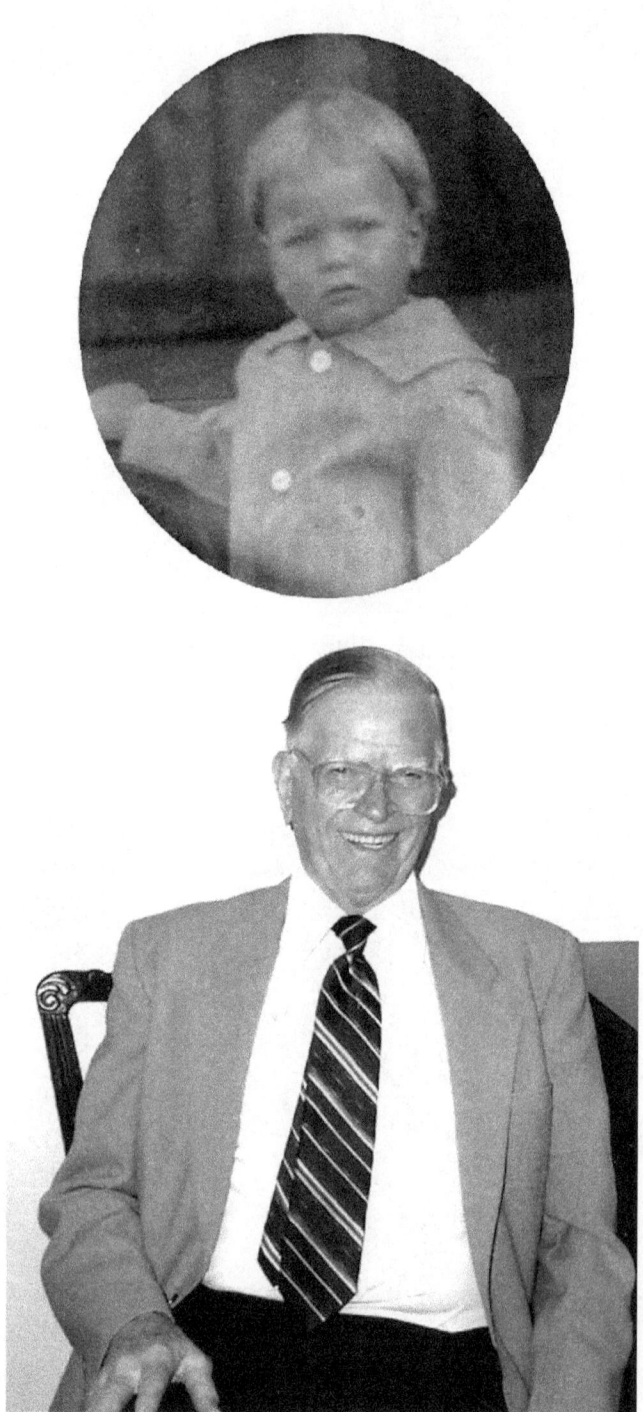

James (Jimmy) Edward Rodgers

The Rodgers & Collins Family

Janice Edwina (Rodgers) Collins
Queen of Chambers County

Travis & Jan's Wedding - July 25, 1964

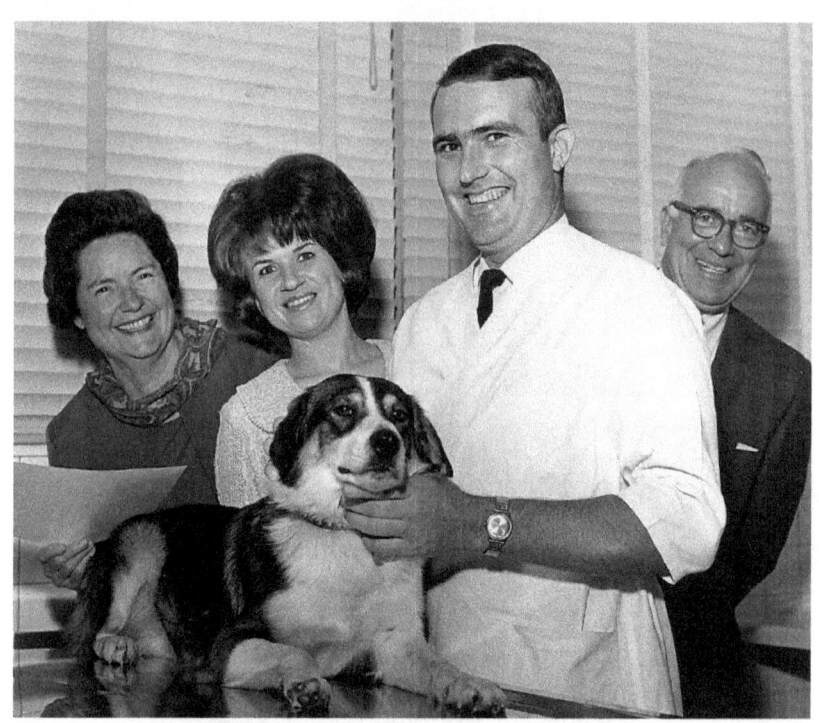

Travis & Jan with Dr. & Mrs. Otto - 1968

Travis & Jason at Collins Family Farm - Utica, Mississippi

Jason Travis Collins

Darryl Lee Rodgers

Darryl & Barbara's Wedding - March 20, 1970

Darryl in the LaFayette High School
Homecoming Parade - 1985

Darryl & Jan Performing in New York City

Amanda's College Graduation - May 8, 2008

Amanda & Stephen's Wedding - July 28, 2007

Stephen, Amanda, Nathan, Natalie & Noah Grubbs

# Poetry

**Papa**

He was always loving and giving;
    Always with encouragement,
"When at first you don't succeed –
    Try, try again."
He worked so hard and had so little;
    And would walk that extra mile,
    To help a neighbor in need.

I know we all have failed and come short of the "Glory of God" – but thanks to Jesus Who came to die on the Cross that we can have "forgiveness" and have eternal "life."

I watched my dad grow older
    Year after year…
And I knew how much he loved us
    For he always wanted us near.
I knew the closeness of our family
    And the joys we had known…
The dreams we had shared
    Are the memories I own.
The last three weeks of Dad's life
    I sat by him day after day…
I felt the loneliness without him
    As he slowly slipped away.

Papa, you were the dearest Dad in the entire world. And as I look back and think of the years gone by, I hold a wonderful picture of you framed within my heart. Instead of seeing those big drops of sweat running down your face, I see your face shining as a big bright star. And you are as fresh as the dew upon the grass. You don't look tired anymore – for you are now resting in "Heavenly Peace."

While lifting up your hands
To give God all the Glory and Praise
The Angels come rejoicing –
As they began to gaze;
And beside you stands Jesus
Saying, "Come unto me,
Heaven is so beautiful –
I want you to see."

So rest a little longer, Papa
       For you have no sweaty brow –
       God is taking
       good care of you,
       and He did hear
       your every prayer.

Papa, the evening you left us
       Was too sad to forget;
I know Mama's heart was breaking
       As I looked upon her face…
We all tried to comfort one another
       And within my heart I knew,
God had picked a precious
       flower
To place in Heaven's vase.

*November 1983*

## My Wonderful Mother

Mama, the day you left us
    My world was torn apart –
Everybody did love you so,
    And it really broke my heart.
Even the thought of being without you
    Was more than I could understand –
And how I wish for one more time
    Just to hold your hand.

By your bedside I stood
    All filled with fear and despair –
But hiding my feelings, I talked,
    Wanting you to know I was there.
You were staring into space, and I wondered if
    You saw Jesus holding out His hand –
Saying, "Come unto me, I will give you rest;
    I will take you home with me to a wonderful land."

Mama, you left this old world
    Without a struggle
Because you saw a better place
    To be –
Someday I'll be there with you
    And while we wait for all the others,
We'll sit down and talk together
    You and me…

How sad that hour of parting
    When the doctor said, "I'm sorry,
We did all we could
    But she's gone" –

I know that you are sleeping
    And resting in peace,
But oh, how I miss you Mama –
    Every day –
Now, dear Mama, you have gone

      To pave the path for me,
So when my life is over
      You and Jesus I will see.

When our journey on earth is over
   We'll be together
      With Him forever –
So, I'll just wait and meet you there,
   And trust in God
      And doubt Him never!

    Mama, you were the dearest Mother in the whole wide world, and I loved you with all my heart. As the years have come and gone, time cannot erase the beautiful picture of you framed within my heart. You don't need that ole walker any more – when Jesus took you by the hand, all earthly afflictions were wiped away.

    I can see you now with angels 'round Heaven's Holy Throne. And I can still see your long beautiful hair – it is flowing softly in Heaven's breeze. Your sweet face is the face of an angel.

The loving memory of you, Mama,
   I'll always keep forever;
And your teachings I will abide.
   They give me peace and rest –
So sleep on my darling mother,
   I will forever miss you;
But as you always taught us,
   God knoweth best.

**October 19, 1983**

**My Book**

I am writing a book
      From the pages of my heart;
I hope to teach someone
      a lesson,
        My love to impart.
And if I should stumble
      Along the world's highway,
I'll quickly ask for guidance,
      and strength;
To travel on the upward path –
      God's message to portray.

*April 1, 1990*

## He Loves Us Still

We are to fear no evil
    If obedient to the Father's will—
He loved us so much, He gave
    And He loves us still—
He gave His only begotten Son
    To free us from all strain and stress—
If our cares we give to Him
    And our sins we confess—

When in silence we sit and pray,
    We may feel a touch of His hand—
"My child," He says, "you are mine;
    No debt you owe, that was my plan.
I brought you into the Light of day
    Out of darkness and evil of the night—
That through My Son, you might see
    He is the Way, the Truth, and the Light."

His Mercy and Love so Divine,
    All our trials and troubles will cease—
If we put our trust in Him,
    To see the beauty of His peace—
With Patience and Happiness to find
    In His mercy, grace, and love—
We'll live with Him forever
    In heaven above.

From the cross to the throne
    Jesus paved for us the way—
The vision John had of Him
    Is also ours today—
He holds the keys of hell and death
    Our sins forgiven, for we have been
Washed in the Blood of Jesus,
    And we know that He is the Amen.

*February 21, 1987*

**God's Love**

I know that God will walk
      With me,
When darkness falls beneath
      My feet –
And He will always be
      My strength;
For He measures not His Love
      By height, depth, nor length.

*March 1990*

*"... the Lord is the strength of my life; of whom shall I be afraid?"*
      *Psalms 27:1*

**Thy Will Be Done**

God framed the world
    with His finger tips –
    And flung the stars in space.
He spoke the Word – and all was done
    With His Blessings and His Grace.

Before our journey
    on Earth is finished –
    May our lives truly express,
All the things we've said and done,
    God's Holy Word we confess.

Christ transforms our lives
    to be Beautiful –
    By the power of His Cross,
The joy and peace are ours
    In serving Him – we'll have no loss.

With His own precious blood
    Jesus bought us –
    Not with silver and gold,
He redeemed us from all unrighteousness
    In His Word we are told.

Jesus went into the Garden
    He prayed alone –
    His life on earth – its course had run,
He prayed the cup might pass from Him.
    "Father," He said, "Thy Will, not Mine, be done."

Jesus is the Resurrection
    and the Life –
    Most blessed, most Holy, are His ways,
Whosoever believeth in Him shall never die.
    He is alive – Thy great name we praise.

*March 19, 1987*

**Driving In The Rain**

Driving in the rain, looking through the car glass
    dimly,
the ever-drizzling rain mixed with wind; and fog
    collecting
misty vapors made each curve look like a horse-
    shoe pattern.
Clouds darkened and trees swayed from the wind swirling
    by.
I fought the rain, but suddenly a thought arose
    in me.
I'll not grapple the storm; by the roadside I
    will wait.

Cars splashed on like billows upon the ocean waves;
    I'll wait –
And watch the mountainous clouds as the sun rays
    grow dimly.
I sat there; lightning flashed, and blurred visions passed
    by me.
Black, silver, and gray puffs of clouds began collecting
Across the sky; the setting sun fading and water
    rushing by –
Well occupied, observing the clouds, I saw a turbulent
    pattern.

Moving onto the road again, my thoughts encircling the
    tires wet pattern,
water rippled into the gullies; the clouds seemed to
    wait
upon the redness of the sunset—bringing crimson shadows
    floating by.
Drivers of the cars I could see only dimly;
rhythms of time breathed slowly, and beaded rain-drops
    kept collecting
while the curves took other cars out of sight
    of me.

Reflecting on many years ago, when my dad, mom,
    and me
Rode along this road, unpaved, even the ruts made
    a pattern.
Moving slowly on—memories to recall, my mind vaguely
    collecting
Thoughts from the past; time goes not backward nor
    will wait;
for time is endless—and my every thought fogs
    my mind dimly.
Gone are the years—my, how time has gone
    by!

I recalled my childhood home; to which I'll never
    say good-bye.
It brought echoes of laughter from lips, now, long
    silent to me;
and the hills that I once climbed, I envision
    only dimly;
but God's hill I'll climb, for He has made
    a wondrous pattern
by His hand and spoken Word; and I will
    wait
on Him to lead me there—for eternal treasures
    I'm collecting.

The storm most battled is within; the memories I'm
    collecting:
I see my dad standing tall, and mom, petite,
    standing by;
a standard they set before me was truly worth
    the wait.
When home again, peace and serenity will come to
    me –
And when I look back on reflections of yesteryears'
    pattern,
I'm entranced by an old treasured picture—colors fading
    dimly.

Driving in the rain, thoughts collecting while dusky shadows
    surround me.
By the long hours of wait—on Heaven's brow,
    an endless pattern
of reflected stars shine through a misty sky dimly.

*July 1987*

"Driving In The Rain" is a sestina. A sestina is a lyrical fixed form consisting of six six-line usually unrhymed stanzas in which the end words of the first stanza recur as end words of the following given stanzas in a successively rotating order and as the middle and end words of the three verses of the concluding tercet.

**Man's Best Friend**

Jesus walked this earth
    So long ago,
In the flesh of man;
    And the message He gave then
Is still so true today,
    And it's going forth throughout the earth
    To fulfill His plan.
    Another Comforter was His promise,
The Holy Spirit He did send;
    And He lives in the hearts of those
    Who will let Him be their friend.

*"And I will pray the Father, and he shall give you another comforter, that He may abide with you forever…*
    *John 14:16*

**A Review**

Yesterday is already memories
    For whatever they may be;
And tomorrow is only a dream,
    Expect it with happiness
    And don't let it flee.
Today is now,
    Live it so you may review;
Every yesterday with beautiful
    memories,
And every tomorrow to be
    a dream come true.

*March 1990*

## Raindrops Falling

I feel a misty breeze
    Upon my face,
As I sit in the cool of the night.
    In the distance –
    Sweet music sounds,
As the whippoorwill calls
    To her mate in shrill delight.

The moon rains out her beams
    Across the sky,
From dusk to the setting sun.
    Clouds brightening –
    Over the horizon,
And heavenly stars peeping
    Through clouds that float and run.

The singing bird
    Is heard no more,
As the night closes out the light of day.
    Raindrops falling –
    While rain-awaken flowers,
Lift up their heads
    In a dancing sway.

*September 13, 1990*

**Knowing True Rest**

Search into the garden
    Of your soul...
And you will find a rest more priceless
    Than all the gold.
The Master stretches out His loving hand –
    As you will find...
    To give us life that He has promised,
    Full of light and peace of mind.

It's in loving and serving
    That you can truly find...
God giving His blessings of rest and peace,
    His love so divine.
It's abiding under the shadow of the Almighty –
    Reaching for the highest and best...
    And knowing God is our refuge,
    And knowing this is true rest.

***March 1993***

*"My people shall dwell in a peaceable habitation... and in quiet resting-places."*
    *Isaiah 32:18*

## The Beauty of the Snowflakes

I watched the beauty
    Of the snowflakes,
Falling softly to the ground –
    Like bubbles
    Blown into the air,
They go drifting and dancing
    To their destiny,
    And never make a sound.

When we look around us
    And see the wonder working,
Of God's great, creative hand –
    Who could doubt
    He is the Holy One,
With the power to perform –
    All the mysteries and the miracles,
    All across this land!

*March 1993*

*"Thou art the God that doest wonders!"*
    *Psalms 77:14*

**Beauty of the Night**

As darkness trails over the
        setting sun,
A hush falls over slumbering
        woods;
Stars come dancing –
Escaping the stillness of the night
        with twinkling lights.
Moon beams burst forth
        in radiant beauty
            Gazing above these high horizons –
Behold the wonder of the hinds' feet;
        Rising beautifully above the earth –
        To soar higher and higher
        Above God's lovely plain.

*March 1990*

*"He maketh my feet like hinds' feet, and setteth me upon my high places..."*
        *Psalms 18:33*

**God's Promises Are True**

If we are weary and troubled
      and do not understand,
We must refuse to be discouraged
      and trust God's Guiding Hand…
We need to remember –
      to have faith in God's Great Love,
And know each day that we live
      is controlled by God Above…
Never dread Tomorrow
      for whatever it may bring,
Just live Today and pray for strength and courage
      and trust God in everything…
Remember His promises are always true
      and on His Word we can depend;
He Promised us Salvation
      and a Life that has no End!

*May 1993*

*"And this is the promise that he hath promised us, even eternal life."*
      *I John 2:25*

**Sufficient Grace**

God walks beside us
Day by day,
And guides us with
        sufficient grace…
If by faith
We'll trust in Him,
All our transgressions and sins
He will forgive
        And will erase.

*March 1993*

**Believe**

If tomorrow is a day of sorrow,
    I will still believe
That God is greater than
    any sorrow.
If I never see answers to my prayers,
    I will still believe
Because God's promises will
    be fulfilled.
God is my refuge
    and my strength.

**To Give and Forgive**

God has no need of our possessions
He owns the earth,
      And everything that's in it.
He owns all the gold and the silver;
      The cattle on a thousand hills.
He loved us –
      Before we were born,
And He loves us still.

God has need of us to be
His earthen vessels,
      To make someone's life anew.
Our example is blazing a trail;
      Each day that we live.
He needs us –
      To be faithful and true,
To love, to give, and forgive.

**God's Hand**

God reached down from Heaven
      And with a gentle touch
      of His hand…
He made the earth a table
      And with grace spread
      Out His Plan…
All the promises God had made
      Was written so plain to see…
And every one of them
      Was meant for you and me.

**Mother's Beauty**

Her beauty was nothing less
Than kind and gentle,
For beauty lies beyond
The house of the soul—
And wings its way to the heart.

I see her as a garden
      forever in bloom;
From spring to summer
And through the autumn days.
As she traveled through the
      field of life—
She scattered seeds of love and kindness
      along the way.

Her beauty was seen in
      all her ways;
A quiet spirit revealed the silent knowledge
      of the unknown.
You could almost know her thoughts and
      unspoken words;
In the silence of her soul,
Whose loving peace was kept from
      dawn to dawn.

**A Silhouette of My Dad**

I saw my dad in the distant field;
    He plowed till he heard the
    night bird's call.
Standing tall against his plow,
    Gazing across the field –
I saw a silhouette of him
    From the windows of the sunset.
Another day's work was done;
    And the smell of freshly plowed earth
    Filled the air –
    As the dew began to fall.

*March 1990*

**God Made Man**

God is the Potter –
And with His hand He fashioned
      the clay of old;
Then finished all His works
      that He had planned.
He saw everything that He had made
      was very good –
And with one sacred breath,
He made man a living soul.

God placed man –
In a garden He so beautifully
      designed.
He planted every tree to be good
      for food;
Except the tree of knowledge –
      it was of good and evil.
Then Satan appeared on the scene
      with deceitful words,
To destroy God's promises so divine.

*"So God created man in his own image…"*
      *Genesis 1:27*

## Temptation

The man called Adam –
And his wife,
      he named Eve,
Were disobedient to the laws
      of God.
By temptation they both
      did sin;
They ate the fruit of the
      forbidden tree,
And from the garden they had to leave.

With the loss of Eden –
God sent one greater
      Man,
To restore and regain
      that blissful seat;
So death could not conquer
      the world.
And with love so abounding,
Jesus came to fulfill God's plan.

*March 27, 1990*

## The Second Adam

God is watching over His own;
> They cannot be plucked
> out of His hand.

He sent Jesus to die
> on the Cross,
> > To take back what the enemy
> > had stolen from man.

Jesus was the second Adam;
> He came to save
> and to heal mankind.

No sin too great for forgiveness
> To those who follow Him.

He raised the dead –
> He healed the lame – the lepers,
> and the blind.

*March 1990*

*"And I give unto them eternal life; and they shall never perish, neither shall any man pluck them out of my hand."*
> *John 10:28*

**Jesus Is Alive**

Jesus is the One, sent from God—
    Whom sin could not contaminate…
He is the One, crucified, risen, reigning,
    and returning—
    Whom death could not hold
But could only claim the victory
    and celebrate…
He is the One, the only One—
    On that first Easter Morn'…
Gave believers hope and the promise
    of eternal life,
    All whom would be reborn…
He is the One, the Beginning and
    the End—
Whom the grave could not
    deprive…
Of proving to the world
    He is Jesus Christ, King of kings
    and Lord of all,
The Son of the living God—
    And He is Alive!

*October 1993*

**Gift of God's Love**

"The earth is the Lord's
    And the fullness thereof"–
God wanted man to subdue the land…
    And to enjoy its fruits;
So as a gift of His Love,
    God gave the earth to man…
With hopes that man would take
    Dominion,
    To share together God's goodness
And do His commands…
    But instead –
Man tried to recreate God's work;
    Only to find he's imprisoned by
    His own greedy hands…
And with all his selfish schemes,
    Man destroyed his blessings;
Who, in his own self-will, resisted
    God's Beautiful Plan!

*"The earth is the Lord's and the fullness thereof; the world, and they that dwell therein"*
    Psalms 24:1

**Compassion**

Stand in the light of God's Word
      And obey Him from above…
Serve Him more faithfully
      And show others of His Love.

Pray in the light of God's Word
      And praise His Holy Name…
You'll find He's never changing –
      His love, mercy and compassion
      always the same.

Listen in the light of God's Word
      And you will hear Him say…
"You are my child – I will never
      leave thee."
So be willing to repent, and
      wait not another day.

Now let us help those in need;
      Do service for Christ while
      we live…
Lift up the fallen and bring
      hope anew,
To poor, lonely people, His
      comfort to give.

**Faith**

What is faith?
Faith is like a light
    Blazing a trail
    through the darkness;
For the rest of the world
    to see –
    Not with the eyes
But with the heart;
    It will shine through
    eternity.

What is faith?
Faith is like a seed
    When planted deep
    And watered well;
It will grow and grow –
    If the roots are grounded
    In good soil,
The harvest fruit will
    overflow.

*March 1990*

*"Now faith is the substance of things hoped for, the evidence of things not seen."*
    *Hebrews 11:1*

**Grandeur Style**

While in silence
     My thoughts to impart
     I painted a masterpiece
     Within my heart.

Softly, the brushes
     Of yesteryears' memories unfold
     Streaked across the canvas
     With a destiny to hold.

A light shining forth
     Danced with freedom so mild
     A priceless work completed
     In grandeur style.

## The Scrapbook Of My Heart

My sister and I
        Were two little bare-
        foot girls…
We ran the fields and the meadows
        Catching grasshoppers and butterflies;
        When we played we were happy
        and free –
        Always felt on top of
        the world…

We both had blue eyes
        Her hair curled, mine was straight as
        could be…
We had our picture taken
        Beside the old gardenia bush,
        The camera man stood under an old
        black cloth –
        To snap a picture of my sister
        and me…

When to bed at night we'd go,
        We never forgot to say
        our prayer…
Out came the crickets and the July flies
        To ring out tunes into the night,
        Daybreak came and they
        were gone –
        Gone in hiding; we knew
        not where…

The coming of spring always brought pleasure
        In the freshness and radiance of
        little showers…
We loved the country and the kindness of earth
        The wild honeysuckle scented air to breathe,
        And colorful butterflies
        to catch –

    Only to release, again, among the
    pretty flowers…

We had a wash hole down on the creek
    We had fun, you
    would agree…
The kids all around came to play
    Town ball, hopscotch, pitching horse shoes,
    Down to the creek we'd soon
    be gone –
    To swing on a vine from the
    Tallest tree…

I can still see
    Our old cotton field so
    long ago…
The hail storm came in raging madness
    Lightning flashed and the thunder roared,
    Then a sudden ray of sun beamed across a
    barren field –
    And shining forth across the sky, a
    beautiful rainbow…

We looked across the storm-torn field
    The cotton was ruined by
    the hail…
Thinking of the debts we owed
    And counted on the cotton crop to pay,
    We would gather what we could
    come fall –
    And, being farmer folks, we knew we
    wouldn't fail…

Thinking of all the yesteryears
    The closeness of our home right from
    the start…
Walking to school each day
    And running to hide if a car came by,
    Picking many-colored hosts of flowers

in spring –
All are memories in the scrapbook of
My heart…

***March 1985***

## To Jason, With Love, Genmo

Your little horse was made of wood,
    You rode him every time you could.
He didn't rock – he had wheels that
    made him go;
    He was your first love – and you could
    ride him fast or slow.

He was given to you from me, your genmo,
    You sure loved me – I did know.
I told you little stories with continuing
    episodes;
    About Fido, a dog that talked – and things
    he did were mighty bold.

This little dog's adventures delighted you so;
    When you rode your horse, you wondered why
    Fido couldn't go.
    Being only two – you thought your horse
    was such a thrill;
    And even at three – you really thought this
    little dog was real.

You have put your first love away;
    He's tucked in a place where he will stay.
All the little stories I told you –
    when in bed;
    They are tucked away also –
    in your head.

*February 1990*

**Little Granddaughter  
To Amanda With Love,  
Grandmother**

Little granddaughters
    Are like snowflakes;
No two exactly alike
    In sizes nor shapes.
You are so smart and precious
    At three years old,
Remembering the things
    You have been told.
Your mind is working
    Like a little computer;
And the words you are saying
    Just couldn't be cuter.
You are a blessing
    – sent from above;
And life wouldn't be complete
    Without having you to love.

*February 1990*

**Treasured Memories**

The happiest of memories to
        recall –
Are the ones my family and I shared
        When I was very
        small –

You know it's hard to remember
        All the things I said and
        did –
For you see my mom and dad
        Always took an interest
        In the lives of all their
        kids –

But one thing I do remember
        Even to this
        day –
I worried about dying
        And would I go to Heaven,
        My mom always smiled and said
        "Yes, God will show you the
        way" –

She taught me the little prayer
        "Now I lay me down to
        sleep" –
And even now as the years go by
        I find myself still praying
        "The Lord my soul to
        keep" –

They have passed away now,
        My mom and
        dad –
But they were just the best
        That any children could have
        had –

I have a family now all my
    own –
I watched my children grow and play
    And all so soon they too were
    gone –

I thank my God
    They found good help-
    mates –
They have good homes
    A husband and wife
    And all is going well, no bitter, no
    hate –

A very precious grandchild
    That filled our hearts with
    joy –
We said, "The good Lord always knows
    If to give a girl or
    boy" –

I've been told there's no difference
    Between a grandchild than your
    own –
And I, too, can truly say,
    They fill an empty place
    In my house anytime when I'm
    alone –

Now I know I'm getting older,
    But I feel that God
    Will use me more if I don't
    fret –
I want to be ready if Jesus should call
    But I'd like to still linger
    For there's more work to do
    yet –

As I grow in years,
> I pray the Lord I'll grow in
> grace –

For when this life on earth is finished
> I want to meet my Savior
> And talk with Him face to
> face.

*June 6, 1983*

## The Beauty of Spring

Each spring is a new beginning –
    A beautiful time of year;
The winter-silent little voices
    We'll soon begin to hear.
Even the tiniest glow-worms
    Illuminate the darkest night,
While other creeping things of earth
    Are chirping with delight.

Walking through the forest and across old hills
    In the early morning dawn,
The wild honeysuckle scented air to breathe,
    Childhood memories unfold – all my own.
A fence still stands – where I had climbed
    To get a surprising view of things;
The many-colored host of flowers to certify
    The beauty of the countryside in spring.

I sat down to rest awhile
    In the cool shade of a giant oak tree,
And I began to picture God
    Among the hills – there with me.
Looking into the distant fields and meadows,
    I saw God in everything;
He spoke through the songs of the birds; He
    smiled in the flowers,
And then, there flew across my heart –
    thanks for another day of spring.

*January 1990*

**The Four Seasons**

God is in all our seasons,
    from spring to summer
    and through the autumn days,
    He makes the north wind blow…
    bringing in winter
    and capping the mountain tops
    white with snow.

We see Him smiling in the flowers,
    rising and waving
    His hands in the trees…
    we hear Him
    through the songs
    of the birds
    and the hum of the bees.

We see Him walking in the clouds,
    outstretching His arms
    in the lightning
    and descending in the rain…
    knowing all this,
    His wonder yet
    cannot be explained.

How do we know God?
    we know Him because –
    He is the God of all creation,
    changeless, the same…
    He says,
    "trust in My love,
    call on My Name."

He threads each day into weeks,
    each week into months,
    the months He grouped together
    for beauty and specific reasons…
    He painted each one
    with a stroke of His hand
    and called them
    the four seasons.

***February 1993***

*"Before the world was formed… from everlasting to everlasting thou art God."*
*Psalms 90:2*

## A Farewell To Santa

Once there was this little old lady,
Whose mind kept leading her astray;
When she talked to me, I just listened
To what she had to say.
She said, "I guess ole Santa must be living;
I haven't seen his name among the dead,
Though I'm getting more forgetful
And more mixed up in the head."

"Christmastime," she said, "Doesn't seem the same
As it did a hundred years before."
"Now, don't get me wrong," she said, my age may be
Less than I think—or could it be even more?
But it's not my age that's bothering me,
It's my mind instead—
Sometimes I can't remember if I'm retiring,
Or if I'm just getting out of bed."

This little old lady wondered what was wrong;
She thought, and thought, and thought again—
"Is it almost Christmas?
Where in the world have I been?"
"Now," she said, "when old Santa comes to town,
To my house he'll surely stop to see
If I've been bad or good—
Or did I forget my Christmas tree."

"Now, I wouldn't want old Santa
To see what's left of me when I get into my bed—
I take out my teeth, and one glass eye,
And the wig from off my head."
Then she thought, "I'll just set Santa's snack
Right near the Christmas tree—
And if he comes to visit,
Surely he won't see me."

Sure enough, Santa slipped down the chimney,
And just as he reached the food and the drink,
Something from her bedroom
Gave him a sudden wink.
Curiosity drew him to the spot
From whence came the sparkle in the night;
But what he saw when he came close
Gave him quite a fright!
He saw an eye staring straight at him
And teeth that grinned with glee;
Presents were forgotten—the only thing on his mind
Was how quickly he could flee!

He scrambled around to find his way out,
His heart pounding with fear—
His only hope for escape
Was to reach his sleigh and his faithful reindeer.
In his haste to retreat
Presents dropped from his sack,
No time to retrieve them—
And he wasn't coming back!

*December 1991*

## A Sequel To A Farewell To Santa

Remember the little old lady
Who slept while Santa fled—
Well it's almost Christmas time again.
And this time, she's not in bed.
While Santa packs the toys and gifts for
      a long winter ride,
He thinks back on his frightful visit
      of the year before—
"I do declare," he said, "I'll not pass
      that house again,
Nor would I dare go in that door."

This forgetful little old lady
Decided that she must move—
Her neighborhood is riddled with crime;
Some things she says, "I can prove"—
So now, she must write to Santa,
And tell him what to bring and give
      her new address—
By the time she finished writing,
She was so tired—she really needed to rest.
But it was almost noon, and she must
      hurry to meet the mail;
There in the cold, she stood beside the mail box,
      her face so very red—
Instead of mailing Santa's letter,
She opened it instead.

Standing there, very confused, wondering
      what to do;
"Now Santa will never know that I have
      moved and live alone"—
In her letter she told him, "I always
      Hear strange noises,
In this old house I call home.

So please, bring me a hi-tech BB gun;
And just place it near my bedroom door—
Cause I tried to decorate a tree,
But that thing fell over and knocked me
        flat to the floor."

Well, Santa did not get the message;
And tomorrow will be Christmas Eve—
All the reindeer are prancing
Getting restless and anxious to leave.
But just what Santa doesn't know,
He's going to be caught in a frightening trap,
For this little old lady will be waiting
Because she will already have had
        her noon-day nap.

Well, ole Santa reached her house very
        unaware of things;
He stood outside, his mind in doubt—
"I don't believe anyone lives here," he said,
But he crept right in very slowly, wanting to be
        sure he could find his way out.
Looking around, being quiet as a mouse,
He saw this flickering little light—
Moving on quietly, trying to see in the dark,
When all of a sudden he saw this
        ungodly sight.

A little old lady sat on a stool;
Combing a wig upon her knee—
His eyes got big and his mouth flew open,
He remembered last Christmas, and again was
        preparing to flee.
"Now, just what did this mean?
Could this little old lady have a twin?"
No sooner had he thought when this bald head
        looked at him and smiled;
And when he saw those great big teeth,
        he recognized that grin.

Now ole Santa had had enough of this;
He started to run but froze in his tracks—
All the toys were scattered on the floor,
And beside him lay an empty sack.
This little old lady started after him;
His foot slipped and he fell down
        on one knee—
And the only thing that he could say,
Was, "Lord have mercy on me!"

## The Exodus

With man's first disobedience, came the very essence of
    Exodus
into God's creation—withdrawing and charging the utmost
    union
of man and woman that brought death into the
    world—and etched
into the Universe pride and envy to all mankind.
    But the Rock
of all Ages stood aloft—arms encircling the avenues
    of the Cross
to come—to save the lost and keep His
    Word unbroken.

The all-seeing Eye—overlooking the plains of Heaven,
    unbroken
by the Stygian food; then the event of the
    Exodus
battling calamity with hope for the Promised land—and
    to cross
the barrier of dire circumstance into a more perfect
    union
of Heaven's perpetual King—and put to proof—He's
    the Rock
of foundation; in His Book saved ones' names are
    deeply etched.

Heaven hides not the Light from our view, but
    etched
The stars in space—and the promise by the
    rainbow—unbroken,
hangs upon the clouds; God reigns firm as the
    Rock
He sent; conquering Satan with one great event, and
    bringing Exodus
into reality and justifying the ways of the union
between God and man—to come by the way
    of the Cross.

The infernal Serpent—deceiving the mother of mankind, but
    the Cross
of one greater Man to come—and whose name
    to be etched
into the "Pages of Time"—regain that blissful
    union
of Genesis when God blessed man and gave unbroken
laws; Satan's rebellion had blazed him out of Heaven
    –dispersing Exodus
–exalting himself "equal to the Most High"—rapidly descending
    as a rock.

God, in His Omnipotent love—built His Church upon
    the Rock;
the Chief Cornerstone who accepted death—transforming life
from
    the Cross.
A deceiving kiss loss happened and gave lasting pain—
    weaving Exodus
of the inner man to grow in wisdom—knowledge
    etched
in inspired understanding—uniting a flow of unity with
    harmony unbroken—
bringing prayerful communion upon a Royal Priesthood of
    Holy union.

Guiding His people by way of cloud and fire—
    the precious union
of God and man grew in awesome events—setting
    the true Rock
to move with passion—for we are fashioned of
    clay unbroken—
and guided by the loving hand of the Unseen
    The Cross
is our salvation—and the fullness of God etched
in us the unlimited promises given through the Exodus.

With creation and disobedience of man, etched into the
    world—a union
of Genesis and Exodus—expounding the Lamb's Passover.
    The Rock
of all eternity—hung upon the Cross with awesome
    victory—unbroken.

***October 1987***

## The Light

Christ did calm the storm
And said unto the sea, "Peace be still" –
That's why He says to you and me,
"Fear not, my Word is my will –
Follow after righteousness
With all your soul and might –
My Word is a lamp unto thy feet,
And unto thy path a light."

**From My Heart To Yours**

I loved you yesterday…
        And trusted completely in your love.
I love you today…
      Because in trusting,
      I learned to love you more.
I know that God brought us together,
      With love that will never grow old –
I will love you tomorrow…
      For all the beautiful memories
      You have given,
      Reach even deeper than the soul!

*Happy Anniversary Darling*
*With All My Love*
*Thelma*
*1939 – September 16 – 1989*

**To A Wonderful Husband On Our
50th Wedding Anniversary
1939 – September 16th – 1989**

Dear Jimmy,

The special memories of yesterday
  Are those when you and I first met,
  And love began to grow…
Your tender loving care,
  So complete,
  Made known the feelings
  Words just could not show.

The happy memories of the past
  Are with me still;
  I hope you know…
Because the world's best man
  Is still,
  As you were then,
  My best beau.

I remember when we were married,
  September sixteenth, in the year,
  Nineteen hundred thirty-nine…
Love so wonderful –
  God brought us together;
  The years we've shared
  Are precious moments of time.

Yes, we said our wedding vows,
  "In sickness and in health,
  Rich or poor…"
We've lived our vows,
  And I can truly say,
  "God is our guide – and of His Word
  We are a doer."

We'll celebrate our 50$^{th}$ Wedding Anniversary
    September sixteenth, in this year,
    Nineteen hundred eighty-nine…
Loving and sharing –
    A lifetime together;
    We become as one,
    Your heart and mine.

We've shared our joys and laughter,
    We've shared our concerns
    From within…
I'll say now,
    As many times before,
    Our closeness still remains,
    The way it's always been.

We have had fifty wonderful years
    Spent together,
    And dreams come true –
We know the best
    In one another;
    We know
    What love can do.

Yes, love has taught us many things
    It's taught us how to live with joy,
    And also tears…
It's made this house of ours
    A home –
    Life would be too short
    If lived a million years.

Time did teach – as did love
    It taught us when to plan
    And when to do…
If we forgot
    The things we shouldn't,
    God was always there
    To see us through.

Old chapters of life behind us –
    New ones to come,
    Yet to be spent…
With each new tomorrow –
    Our strength renewed;
    We'll show what our love,
    Our patience has meant.

The pages of time turn on –
    A new page,
    A new day…
And as we grow older,
    Our steps more slowly,
    We'll cherish each moment,
    Holding hands along the way.

This is a beautiful time in our lives
    To rejoice in the Lord,
    To thank Him forever…
For all His gifts –
    And love so divine,
    And thank Him for the special way
    His plan brought us together!

***Your loving wife,***
    ***Thelma***

*A thank you to attendees of our 70<sup>th</sup> Anniversay Tea.*

## 70<sup>th</sup> Anniversary
## 1939 – September 16<sup>th</sup> – 2009

We thank each of you
For sharing in our joy today –
You have helped us celebrate
Our 70<sup>th</sup> wedding anniversary
In a very special way –
We'll only do this once in life,
And it blesses us to know –
That we have friends who care enough
To drop in just to say "hello."

We hope you signed our anniversary book,
Each name we'll read when the day is spent –
Those who came – and those who served;
You'll never know what it has meant –
This is a special time in our lives and will be
Memories in our heart to stay –
And as we wake with each tomorrow
We'll give thanks for another day!

***From Our Hearts To Yours,***
***Thelma and Jimmy***

**Remember**

Some of the happy memories
    I'd like to
    recall –
Are the ones you and I shared
    When we were very
    small –

Remember when…
    We were two little girls
    Happy as could
    be –
    Walking to school each day,
    Up hill, down hill, to Red Hill you
    see –

Remember when…
    Upon the grasses we shared our lunch
    Out of a little brown
    bag –
    Then all the girls ran and played
    Dropping the handkerchief and a game called
    tag –

Remember when…
    We'd climb the tallest tree
    That thrust into the
    skies –
    A child we were, filled with laughter
    And summer in our
    eyes –

Remember when…
    Too speedily, too swiftly,
    Our childhood summit
    won –
    We'd climbed the last tall tree
    That leans into the
    sun –

Remember when…
    We were teenagers
    Dating and having
    fun –
    One Hill behind us
    And another one to
    run –

Remember when…
    Your dad and my dad played the banjo,
    The music started and the square dance was
    called –
    Swing her to the right, swing her to the left,
    Swing your partner, promenade
    all –

Remember when…
    At Union Hill School we came,
    Red Hill far behind
    us –
    We no longer had to walk
    But now could ride a
    bus –

Remember when…
    We left the Hills,
    Launching out – when to anchor we did not
    know –
    To LaFayette we came to finish high school
    And that was fifty years
    ago –

Remember when…
    You and John first met,
    Love so strong, the blossom-scented
    air –
    Good friends to share your laughter and tears,
    No two could have made a better
    pair –

Remember when…
>All is said and done,
>You and John have fifty wonderful
>years –
>Spent together, loving and caring,
>Always sharing moments of joy and
>tears –
>There is not time, now, in the crowded years
>To stop the time nor halt the
>pace –
>But as we grow in years
>Let's pray the Lord we'll grow in
>grace –

***June 28, 1986***
***In honor of Edna and John Robinson's 50th Wedding Anniversary***

## To Pearl Cain – A New Friend

When we were growing up
        And still so very
        small –
We lived miles apart
        And didn't know each other at
        all.

If you were a child like me
        You ran and played under the beautiful
        skies –
A child I was, filled with happiness
        And love of nature in my
        eyes.

If we had known each other then
        We could have had
        fun –
We would have played from early morn'
        Till the setting of the
        sun.

Too speedily, too swiftly
        My childhood days were
        spent –
Old chapters of life behind me
        New ones that God has
        sent.

The pages of time turn on
        A new page – a new friend I'd
        met –
I thank God that life is so precious,
        The friendship we've made, I'll never
        forget.

Fond memories of bygone days
    Are still to me so very
    near –
Old friends to remember – new ones,
    All whom I hold so
    dear.

A true friend is hard to find
    And I can truly
    say –
I'm glad we met some years ago
    I'm glad you are my friend
    today.

Remember when…
    We married our guys
    In the year, nineteen hundred
    thirty nine –
Years later – God brought us all together
    Wonderful friends to know, just two of a
    kind –
We'll celebrate our 50$^{th}$ wedding anniversary
    In this year, nineteen hundred
    eighty nine –
Gene and yours – Jimmy and
    mine.

**In Memory Of Gene Cain**

Gene Cain is a sturdy man,
    Tall of stature and handsome 'tis true –
His education at Berry College,
    Brought many memories to share
    with me and you.

Each Sunday he and his lovely wife, Pearl,
    Worship at First Baptist Church
    Before lunch –
Afterwards they meet old friends
    at Rodger's Restaurant,
      And while they are there, they visit
      a bunch.

Gene knows the Lord personally,
    He enlightens us about the Word
    with pride –
Speaking with kindness in his voice,
    With eighty-two Novembers in his eyes.

Gene has a real trade mark,
    When you see him on Sunday he'll
    be wearing a colorful bow-tie –
He greets the people with a cheerful
    smile,
    For he's never met a stranger
    nor ever been shy.

This man believes in living life to
    its fullest,
    He has a mind that is very keen –
And he's always joking with all
    of his friends,
      Remembering the eighty-two Novembers
      he has seen.

There is one thing we must not forget,
>   How Gene likes to hunt with his
>   fox hounds at night –
If his dogs could talk, they might have
>   lots to tell,
>>  When Gene comes home in the
>>  morning's light.

He drives his truck into the woods,
>   He sits and listens with eagerness
>   in his face –
His fox hounds bark, bringing music
>   to his ears,
>>  While gazing to see the moon and the
>>  stars that God flung in space.

Now I haven't told all that I know
>   about Gene Cain,
>>  For he is my friend and some things
>>  I had to keep right from the start –
But one more thing I must say, he
>   has accumulated much wisdom,
>>  In the scrapbook of his heart.

**Friends – Jimmy & Thelma Rodgers**

## A Special Tribute to Dr. Bentley

The narrative that is related here is about a
    little journey we have been on for the past year.
This journey will walk us through the pages
    of Lafayette First Baptist Church—
It's preacher, Brother Jim, for a new flock
    began a diligent search.

Pastor Jim sought and found what appeared
    To be greener pastures elsewhere;
But this is only the beginning of this little story,
    For none could foresee
That in the upcoming "preacher swap"—
LaFayette First Baptist would get the
    "cream of the crop."

The church where Brother Jim was moving
    had lost its preacher by retirement;
Little did this pastor know there would be no rest;
    but being obedient,
He has faithfully continued here as God's
    instrument of peace—
Ministering with grace and a pure heart,
    helping members their faith to release.

Dr. David Bentley came with an outpouring of love
    and a smile on his face,
Full of wisdom and instructive wit;
He's a giant of a man, not only in
    stature,
But also with a spirit that doesn't quit.

He realizes now that he has not yet emptied
    his spiritual storehouse of divine knowledge.
We are new ground for him to sow,
    needing a firmer foundation—
With sprinkles of humor and discernment,
    he blesses our garden of tender plants,

Swaying our stems—shaking our leaves and planting our roots
        in the rich Godly soil of healthy communication.
Let us pay a special tribute to Dr. Bentley, who
        divinely did not pursue his beckoning call to retire;
For God had another plan—He directed this beloved disciple,
        with his helpmate, on another path yet to be trod—
And a special thanks to our Heavenly Father
For keeping Dr. Bentley's gospel feet shod.

      It has been our privilege to know Dr. Bentley and his lovely wife, Jo, closely for the past year. Knowing Dr. Bentley at this level of his ministry, after preparation for retirement, we have witnessed his prophetic desire for God to keep using him. We see Dr. Bentley pouring forth out of his heart and his communion with the Lord to bless the body of Christ.

      Dr. Bentley, thank you for sharing this time of your life with all of us, for working with us—knowing us well enough to call each one by name. And thank you for giving us a chance to re-evaluate how we are doing at walking worthy of the vocation wherewith we have been called "personally." As one who has been "sent forth" to be the shepherd of a pasture of scattered sheep, we can, therefore, be more humble in closing the gap that may have hindered the fulfillment of God's mission for us.

      We have been stirred toward an even more intimate relationship with the Lord. And it has fanned the flame of a desire we have toward knowing God intimately and in all of His fullness because of the love and fellowship that you, Dr. Bentley, have brought to our church.

So, the pages of God's time turn on—
    A new page, a new day—
May we all rejoice in the Lord,
      To thank Him now and always
      For His Love so divine;
And thank Him for His special plan
      To send Dr. Bentley our way.

***July 19, 1992***

# Poems By
# My Daughter, Edwina

**Learning To Love**

Let Love make your heart sing
    When all your joy is gone.
Let Love find a resting place
    Close to you and you alone.

Let Love awaken you in morning's light,
    And walk in peace all the day.
Let Love indwell your spiritual self
    And keep all wickedness away.

Let Love speak for you
    In all your actions and your deeds.
Let Love cover you with robes of kindness
    To help someone in need.

Let Love fill your soulish self
    To impart to others a helping hand.
Let Love guide your walk this hour.
    And follow Jesus – God's plan for man.

*Given to me by the Holy Spirit*
*Edwina Rodgers Collins*
*March 31, 1991*

## Under The Influence From Mountain Tops

The mountains seem to echo thoughts
As an unseen voice showers down upon me.
Therefore—I write under the influence of feelings—
in tune with my inner-most self.

My mind is at rest as I look up ahead;
I feel a void—tugging in my heart.
Therefore—I write under the influence of feelings—
like a cloud pulling drapes of satin against my flesh.

My soul thinks not on any one thing
As the depths of my spirit thunders loudly across my heart.

There are lonely people
Remembering their lives
Overshadowed by past experiences—
Dressed in robes of tainted memories
Of no more caring—tossed aside—
As voices echoing across the mountains only to be forgotten.

This pierces my inner most self—
Therefore—I write under the influence of feelings.
A warm glow-the color of liquid gold
Fills an emptiness deep down inside
And bathes my spirit of compassion with meekness—
A desire-so forceful—so true—

A churning upward like a mountain of despair
Waiting to release an energy
To envelope these forgotten ones into loving arms of protection and care.
Therefore—I write under the influence of feelings—
While looking at these stately mountains.

I cry out inside—
As a color wheel emerges,
And the moon soon lights each color
Focusing on hues of blue, white, green, and silver—
Soon—the color red will burst forth—
And with its energy change the shades of time
To shadows of new dimensions—

And that radiant liquid gold
Will come and melt the sorrow
Of each soul left to breathe
The air of loneliness.

*Edwina Rodgers Collins*

Joe, Pearl & Mary Jo Stanfield

Stanfield Family Reunion

Jimmy, J.D., Voncile & Hennon Rodgers

Uncle Dewey Stanfield, Aunt Belle Stanfield Moore, Aunt Mag Stanfield Adams, Parrie Lee Stanfield Adams (Mama) & Uncle Ed Stanfield; Not Pictured: Uncle Will Stanfield & Uncle John Stanfield

Gladys, Lorene, Irene & Olivia Amanda
Melvena McClendon (Granny) Adams

Aunt Belle Stanfield Moore, Parrie Lee Stanfield Adams (Mama),
Aunt Mag Stanfield Adams & Eddie Adams

Corbert, Mag & Calvin Adams

Cathleen, Calvin & Thelma Adams

Clyde Adams                     Rogers Adams

PAN-AM Gas Station - Prior to Rodgers Restauarant

Minnie Pearl Rodgers

Corbert, Lorene, Gladys, Irene, Clyde, Herbert, Roscoe & Brenice Adams

Corbert Adams & Edwina Rodgers

Wayland & Barbara Whiddon

Rodgers Home Since 1959

Edna (Adams) Jackson & Clayton Sims

Bennie, Sonya (Adams), Bryan Lee & Tamara Yates

Myrtle (Cline) Adams, Bennie & Sonya (Adams) Yates,
Cheryl (Adams) Landrum & Casey Jennings

Bennie & Sonya (Adams) Yates

Billy Turnham

Paul & Grace Easterling

Jimmy, Robin, Jamie & Jimmie Lyn Jackson

Amanda (Rodgers) Grubbs, Amy (Smith) Blackstock
& April (Smith) Freitag

Fred & Voncile Whiddon, Jimmy & Thelma Rodgers
& Amanda Rodgers

Mike & Cindy Smith          Steve & Helen Smith

Buford & Jo Ann Cotton

Allen & Dot Powers

Jimmy's Pontiac in 1956

Sawyer Brown Band at Rodgers Restaurant - 1987

Gene Hackman & Thelma Rodgers
Filming of Mississippi Burning in LaFayette, Alabama - 1988

Adams Family Reunion - November 2, 2013

www.ingramcontent.com/pod-product-compliance
Lightning Source LLC
Chambersburg PA
CBHW032046150426
43194CB00006B/444